CAMPAIGN 386

TANNENBERG 1914

Destruction of the Russian Second Army

MICHAEL McNALLY

ILLUSTRATED BY SEÁN Ó'BRÓGÁIN

Series editor Nikolai Bogdanovic

OSPREY PUBLISHING
Bloomsbury Publishing Plc
Kemp House, Chawley Park, Cumnor Hill, Oxford OX2 9PH, UK
29 Earlsfort Terrace, Dublin 2, Ireland
1385 Broadway, 5th Floor, New York, NY 10018, USA
E-mail: info@ospreypublishing.com
www.ospreypublishing.com

OSPREY is a trademark of Osprey Publishing Ltd

First published in Great Britain in 2022

© Osprey Publishing Ltd, 2022

A catalogue record for this book is available from the British Library.

ISBN: PB 9781472850225; eBook 9781472850218; ePDF 9781472850201; XML 9781472850232

22 23 24 25 26   10 9 8 7 6 5 4 3 2 1

Maps by Bounford.com
3D BEVs by Paul Kime
Index by Fionbar Lyons
Typeset by PDQ Digital Media Solutions, Bungay, UK
Printed and bound in India by Replika Press Private Ltd.

Author's note

As always I would like to thank my wife and family for their continued support through what – on occasion – has been a difficult writing progress. Also words of thanks to Seán Ó'Brógáin for interpreting my words and notes and from them creating the three colour plates which accompany the text; to my editor, Nikolai Bogdanovic, for his patience and words of encouragement when things became difficult; and finally to Nik Cornish for allowing me to take up the baton.

Artist's note

Readers may care to note that the original paintings from which the colour plates in this book were prepared are available for private sale. All reproduction copyright whatsoever is retained by the publishers. All enquiries should be addressed to:

seanobrogain@yahoo.ie

The publishers regret that they can enter into no correspondence upon this matter.

Osprey Publishing supports the Woodland Trust, the UK's leading woodland conservation charity.

To find out more about our authors and books visit **www.ospreypublishing.com**. Here you will find extracts, author interviews, details of forthcoming events and the option to sign up for our newsletter.

A note on unit abbreviations

In this work, battalions of regiments are referred to using Roman numerals, e.g. II./Infanterie-Regiment 150 (2nd Battalion, 150th Infantry Regiment). Companies within regiments are referred to using Arabic numerals, e.g. 12./Infanterie-Regiment 150 (12th Company, 150th Infantry Regiment).

Gazeteer of place names

Many of the place names relating to the events of the Battle of Tannenberg have changed radically since 1914. The following list is intended to help the reader locate significant places associated with the battle by their modern names.

Name used in text	Modern name	Country
Allenstein	Olsztyn	Poland
Angerburg	Wegorzewo	Poland
Bartenstein	Bartoszyce	Poland
Benkheim	Banie Mazurskie	Poland
Bialystok	Bialystok	Poland
Danzig	Gdansk	Poland
Darkehmen	Osyorsk	Russia
Enzuhnen	Ckalovo	Russia
Goldapp	Goldap	Poland
Graudenz	Grudziadz	Poland
Gumbinnen	Gusev	Russia
Heidenburg	Grodzisko	Poland
Hohenstein	Olsztynek	Poland
Insterburg	Tschernachowsk	Russia
Königsberg	Kaliningrad	Russia
Kovno	Kaunas	Lithuania
Kraupisken	Uljanowo	Russia
Lötzen	Gizyko	Poland
Lyck	Elk	Poland
Marienburg	Malbork	Poland
Memel	Klaipeda	Lithuania
Mlawa	Mlawa	Poland
Ortelsburg	Szczytno	Poland
Ossowjez	Osowiec	Poland
Pillkallen	Dobrowolsk	Russia
Rominten	Krasnolesye	Russia
Stallupönen	Nesterov	Russia
Szirgupönen	Dalneje	Russia
Thorn	Torun	Poland
Tilsit	Sowetsk	Russia
Tollmingkehmen	Tschistye Prudy	Russia
Warsaw	Warszawa	Poland

Front cover main illustration: The men of Colonel Otto von Heydebreck's Infanterie-Regiment 146 are confronted by a Russian counter-attack at Hohenstein on 29 August 1914. (Seán Ó'Brógáin)

Title page photograph: A senior German officer decorates soldiers for bravery in the field. (Author's collection)

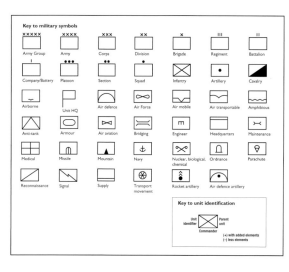

Key to military symbols

Army Group | Army | Corps | Division | Brigade | Regiment | Battalion

Company/Battery | Platoon | Section | Squad | Infantry | Artillery | Cavalry

Airborne | Unit HQ | Air defence | Air Force | Air mobile | Air transportable | Amphibious

Anti-tank | Armour | Air aviation | Bridging | Engineer | Headquarters | Maintenance

Medical | Missile | Mountain | Navy | Nuclear, biological, chemical | Ordnance | Parachute

Reconnaissance | Signal | Supply | Transport movement | Rocket artillery | Air defence artillery

Key to unit identification

Unit identifier — Parent unit
Commander
(+) with added elements
(–) less elements

CONTENTS

ORIGINS OF THE CAMPAIGN

Whilst it often accepted that the assassination of the Archduke Franz Ferdinand von Hapsburg by Serb nationalists in June 1914 was the catalyst for the catastrophe of a global conflict, it was an event that took place almost a quarter of a century before that was to make a general conflict more certain than at any time since the Napoleonic Wars. In March 1890, after lengthy disagreements about Germany's political course, Kaiser Wilhelm II forced the resignation of his long-serving chancellor, Otto, Prince von Bismarck.

Born in the year of Napoleon's defeat at Waterloo, Bismarck would come to stand astride European politics like a colossus. From his initial membership of the Prussian parliament in 1849, his rise would be steady and relentless, with various ambassadorial appointments coupled with political alliances leading to him becoming Minister-President of Prussia at the suggestion of his close friend Albrecht von Roon, the Minister of War. These two, together with Helmuth von Moltke, Chief of the Prussian General Staff, were to form a triumvirate which would ultimately – in the decades to come – transform the Kingdom of Prussia into the German Second Empire.

DROPPING THE PILOT.

In time, both the Second Schleswig War (February–October 1864) and the Austro-Prussian War (1866) would serve to demonstrate one of the templates of Bismarckian Foreign Policy: a short decisive conflict followed by a negotiated settlement, favourable to Prussian/German interests. With these two victories Bismarck not only unified Germany politically, but also resolved the centuries-old rivalry between Hapsburg and Hohenzollern, consigning Austrian interests to Italy and the Balkans, where it would eventually come into conflict with Russia.

Prior to embarking on his war with Austria, Bismarck had obtained France's tacit neutrality with an implied acquiescence to its annexation of Luxembourg. When France demanded that Prussia honour this commitment, it was firmly rebuffed. The situation worsened two years later when the Spanish government offered the vacant throne to the Prince of Hohenzollern-Sigmaringen, a cadet branch of the Prussian ruling house. In view of what it saw as a hostile encirclement, Paris not only reiterated its demands regarding Luxembourg but also called for Prussian acceptance of a return to the borders of 1814, something which the French government knew that Berlin could never, and indeed would never, agree to.

Just as Denmark and then Austria had fallen to Prussian arms, Bismarck, by now Prussian chancellor, was certain that France – seen by many as a destabilizing influence in European affairs – would find precious few allies in the event of open conflict; but the key would be to portray France as the aggressor and Prussia as the injured party. If this could be done, it would undoubtedly facilitate the resolution of another long-standing question, that of France's German-speaking eastern provinces Alsace and Lorraine. Whilst sabres were rattled in Paris, Bismarck was instead entering into discussions with all of the German states, particularly those such as Bavaria and Württemberg, which had previously been allied to Austria. Thus, on 19 July 1870, when France declared war on Prussia and the North German Confederation, it ultimately found itself in a conflict with the whole of Germany.

The French had miscalculated when, in 1866, they stood aside in anticipation of Prussian defeat; this decision now returned to haunt them. Simply put, the French Second Empire was but a shadow of the First, whilst Roon's overhaul and reorganization of the Prussian army meant that the enemy could put more men in the field at a faster rate than France could achieve, and the initial invasion of Germany was soon transformed into a Prussian-led invasion of France characterized by battles of encirclement and manoeuvre for which the French had no real answer. The Imperial government effectively fell with the capture of Emperor Napoléon III at Sédan, and although the war was militarily lost, the fighting would continue until the surrender of Paris on 28 January 1871.

Behind the scenes, however, Bismarck had begun conducting private negotiations not only with the new French government, but also with Prussia's own allies. On 18 January – in the Hall of Mirrors at Versailles – the existing union was effectively consigned to history with the assimilation of all German States, with the exception of Austria, into a new German Empire, the 'Second Reich' under the leadership of Prussia, whose monarch was now acclaimed as Kaiser Wilhelm I, with Otto von Bismarck appointed as Imperial Chancellor.

Hearkening back to the wars of the 19th century, this recruiting poster calls the German Landsturm (militia) to arms. (Author's collection)

General Leonid Artmanov, commander of the Russian I Corps, Second Army. (Wikimedia Commons)

ALLIANCES AND MISALLIANCES

Having won this final conflict, Bismarckian policy now dictated the pursuit of a diplomatic settlement aimed at securing Germany's political position. Acknowledging that Germany would always have three potential rivals in continental Europe, the new chancellor's view was that if he could forge an alliance with two of them, most likely Austria

General Hermann von François, commander of the German I.Armee-Korps, 8.Armee. (Author's collection)

and Russia, then the third, almost inevitably France, would remain bereft of allies – isolated and impotent.

Discussions therefore began with both Vienna and St Petersburg to broker an agreement that would ensure this alliance, whilst maintaining these partners' interests in eastern Europe. This was achieved with the ratification in 1873 of the *Dreikaiserbund* (or League of the Three Emperors), which was aimed at stifling rising nationalism in the region whilst simultaneously resolving potential Austro-Russian rivalries by agreeing their respective spheres of political influence.

With slight modifications, this all-important treaty would form the cornerstone of German foreign policy, remaining in force from 1873 to 1878 and 1881 to 1887, but was ultimately doomed by Austro-Russian conflicts of interest in the Balkans. When it lapsed for the first time in 1878, with Russia emerging victorious from a war with Turkey, Austria and Germany committed themselves to a mutual defence pact known as the Dual Alliance, an agreement later expanded as the Triple Alliance by the addition of Italy as a further counterweight against potential French aggression.

Ultimately, Austro-Russian tensions proved to be incompatible for the continued existence of the alliance and upon its final lapse Bismarck arranged a separate agreement with Russia known as the Reinsurance Treaty, which would come into force should either party be attacked by an – as yet – unknown great power. As Bismarck had no intention of renewing hostilities with France, it was a masterpiece of diplomacy that could have ensured peace in Europe for decades to come. But by June 1888, a succession crisis in Germany had seen the deaths of the 90-year-old Kaiser Wilhelm I and that of his son, the terminally ill Friedrich III, who, on 15 June, was succeeded by the Crown Prince Friedrich Wilhelm, who ascended the throne as Kaiser Wilhelm II.

The son was unlike the father and grandfather. Although Wilhelm I had been overly reliant upon Bismarck, it is generally assumed that had Friedrich III survived his illness, he would have replaced his chancellor sooner rather than later. Such an act would have been undertaken via established practice, but when Bismarck was forced to offer his resignation in spring 1890, it was purely on the grounds that of the two men involved one was 'God's Anointed' and one was not.

Bismarck's departure literally marked a sea change in German diplomacy – rapprochement was in future to be sought not with Russia, but rather with Great Britain, with whom the Kaiser would pursue a fatal love–hate relationship. As a result, when the Reinsurance Treaty was allowed to lapse, France was more than ready to grasp the resulting opportunity with both hands, a promise of extensive French financial investment being more than sufficient to secure the defensive military treaty that only one of the signatories truly desired. Whilst there is some debate as to the importance of the treaty to German foreign policy as a whole, there can be no doubt that its continued existence had successfully kept France neutralized, thus preventing the nightmare scenario of the empire being forced to fight a war on two fronts.

Austro-German and Russian deployments, 28 July 1914

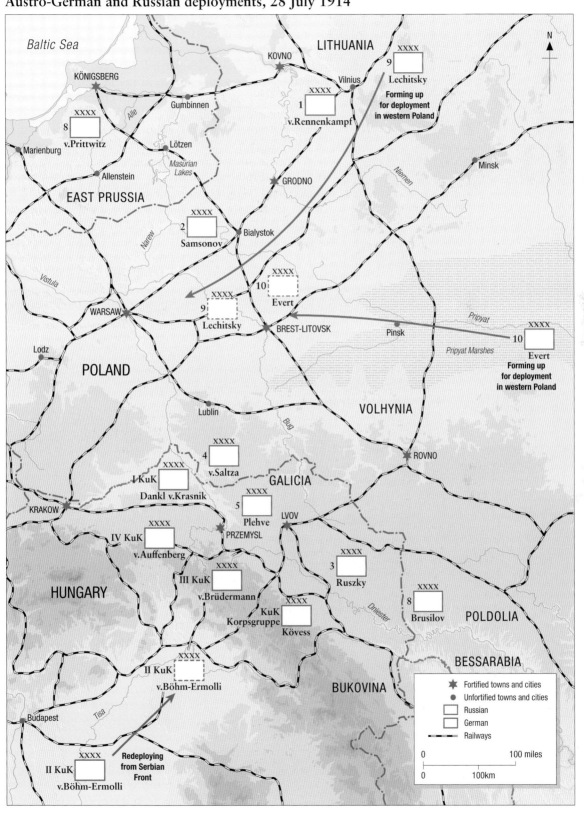

GIRDING FOR WAR

'Home before the leaves fall?' German troops shortly after mobilization, August 1914. (Bundesarchiv, Bild 146-1974-118-18/CC-BY-SA 3.0, CC BY-SA 3.0 DE)

Part-time soldiers: members of the East Prussian Landwehr. (Author's collection)

As the crisis of June 1914 escalated and extended into July, the fate of Europe lay in the hands of two men. One was the 46-year-old Nicholas II Romanov, Tsar of Russia, whose overwhelming conviction lay in the support and defence of both the Orthodox Church and the Slavic Race; the other was his cousin, Wilhelm II von Hohenzollern, Kaiser of Germany, a man whose self-image was such that he was desperate to be seen as both a benevolent modern ruler and as an able military commander in the Prussian military tradition.

Although war was not a certainty, Austria's desire to strike out at Serbia meant that it needed a counterweight to Russia's obvious support, and of its two current allies only one could provide such a guarantee. Berlin's response was a *grand geste*, one typical of its imperial master, who wrote that he would 'stand loyally by Austria-Hungary in accordance with his treaty obligations and in recognition of our old friendship'. Germany would therefore fully support any course of action that Austria decided to undertake against Serbia, whilst simultaneously counselling that Vienna strike hard and fast, in order to capitalize upon international sympathy over the assassination and hopefully bring matters to a successful conclusion before any outside powers – in effect Russia – could intervene.

Armed with this assurance, the Austrian high command made its plans, deciding to conduct a full mobilization before commencing hostilities;

but the Imperial and Royal army was a cumbersome organism, and it was soon clear that this could not be completed before 25 July at the earliest. Accordingly, and as its army began the lengthy process, a detailed ultimatum was sent to Serbia in full expectation of an immediate refusal; but on 28 July – without the knowledge that the Tsar had ordered a partial Russian mobilization in their support – the Serbs accepted most of the Austrian demands.

In Berlin, the Kaiser saw this as another triumph of German diplomacy, commenting that it was, 'A great moral success for Vienna, and with it all reason for war is gone,' adding that 'I would never have recommended mobilization on this basis!'

Despite this unexpected response and following a number of erroneous reports of skirmishes along the border, Austria issued a declaration of war against Serbia the same day. On 30 July, Russia gave orders for a general mobilization. Germany then demanded that St Petersburg immediately halt its preparations, and when this was refused, issued its own declaration of war against Russia on 1 August. It followed this up with a similar announcement against Paris two days later, resulting in a German invasion of northern France and Belgium.

The political dominoes continued to fall, with Great Britain demanding that Belgian neutrality be respected and that German troops withdraw without delay. The ultimatum was ignored, and on 4 August Britain declared war upon Germany. This was closely followed by Austria's declaration of war against Russia on 6 August and Franco-British declarations of war against Vienna six days later. Although the participants' overseas possessions would ensure that the conflict would not be confined to Europe, it only took on a truly global nature with the Japanese declaration of war against Germany on 23 August.

STAVKA PLANS

As all sides followed their respective mobilization plans, Stavka – the Russian High Command – was faced with a choice that would have a profound effect on the conduct of the war as a whole, as its troop concentrations were to be dictated by plans that had been drawn up in 1910 to cater for one of two eventualities.

General Alexander Blagoveschensky, commander of the Russian VI Corps, Second Army. (Wikimedia Commons)

'Plan A', as it had become known, had considered a situation whereby the bulk of the German forces would have been committed to operations in the West and the residue of these forces together with all or most of the Austro-Hungarian army would be committed against Russia. The alternate plan, or 'Plan G', was based upon the supposition that Germany would remain on the defensive in the West and that the bulk of its forces, together with the Austro-Hungarian army, would combine in an attempt to knock Russia out of the war at an early stage before transferring forces westwards as circumstances dictated.

In the first option, the Russian First and Second armies would combine to engage any German forces in East Prussia, with the Third, Fourth and Fifth armies facing off against the Austrians whilst additional armies (Sixth through to Tenth) mobilized. In the second variant, the Russian armies would deploy to contain the German forces in East Prussia whilst the bulk of the combat strength moved against the Austro-Hungarian forces in the Carpathians.

In the end, Stavka elected to adopt 'Plan A', but nonetheless – and in consideration of French political pressure – the Russian First and Second armies, instead of adopting a defensive stance, were directed to invade East Prussia, thus adding another problem to those already plaguing the speed and effectiveness of Russia's mobilization.

CHRONOLOGY

1864	Second Schleswig War. German States are victorious over Denmark.	2 August	Germany declares war on France and Belgium.
1866	Austro-Prussian War. Prussia and Allies are victorious over Austria and its allies.	4 August	Germany invades France and Belgium.
			Britain declares war on Germany.
1870–71	Franco-Prussian War. Prussia and German States are victorious over France. Creation of 'Second German Empire'. King of Prussia becomes German Emperor.	6 August	Austria declares war on Russia.
		12 August	Britain and France declare war on Austria.
1873	League of Three Emperors – *Dreikaiserbund* (1873–78, 1881–87).	17 August	Russian First and Second armies invade East Prussia.
1878	Dual Alliance between Austria-Hungary and Germany (later joined by Italy).		Battle of Stallupönen.
		20–21 August	Battle of Gumbinnen.
1887	Reinsurance Treaty signed between Russia and Germany.	26–30 August	Battle of Tannenberg. Defeat of Russian Second Army.
1888	Accession of Kaiser Wilhelm II.	30–31 August	Remnants of Russian Second Army retreat into Poland.
1890	Bismarck forced to resign as Imperial Chancellor.		
1894	Reinsurance Treaty lapses. France begins overtures to Russia.		

1914

28 June	Assassination of Archduke Franz Ferdinand in Sarajevo.
23 July	Austria mobilizes for war. Ultimatum delivered to Serbia.
28 July	Serbia accepts most of the Austrian conditions.
	Austria declares war on Serbia.
30 July	Russia mobilizes. Germany demands halt to Russian mobilization.
1 August	Germany mobilizes and declares war on Russia.

OPPOSING COMMANDERS

RUSSIAN

General of Cavalry Paul Georg Edler von Rennenkampf (1854–1918)

The son of an army officer, Rennenkampf joined the 89th (White Sea) Infantry Regiment in 1870. After graduating from the Helsingfors (now Helsinki, Finland) Cadet Academy, he joined the 5th (Lithuanian) Ulans. Three years later, he attended the Nikolayev General Staff College in St Petersburg, graduating at the top of his class. The college's principal noted that, 'He has the makings of a fine officer, one who will not fade into the background. Men like him will truly be appreciated when the trumpets sound and the cannon roar.'

Promoted to major in 1882, Rennenkampf spent several years serving in a number of staff and line positions in the Warsaw and Kazan military districts before periods of service with firstly the Don Army and then the II Army Corps, before becoming chief of staff to the commander of the fortress of Ossowjez on the Polish/East Prussian border.

Following a period of regimental service, he became chief of staff to the Transbaikal (or Amur) Military District. During the Boxer Rebellion, he led a mixed column of troops into northern China, gaining a reputation as a brave and capable commander, defeating the local insurgents in a succession of engagements. During the fighting Rennenkampf was twice awarded the George Cross and given command of the 1st Independent Cavalry Brigade.

Paul von Rennenkampf, commander of the Russian First Army. (Wikimedia Commons)

When war broke out with Japan in February 1904, Rennenkampf assumed command of the Transbaikal Cossack Division (later transferring to the Zabaikal Division), during the tenure of which he was elevated to the rank of lieutenant-general.

Badly wounded at the Battle of Liaoyang (24 August– 4 September 1904), he was forced to temporarily relinquish command of his division. One of his officers was Baron Peter Wrangel, a subaltern in the 2nd Transbaikal Cossack regiment, who would later command the White Armies during the Russian Civil War. Wrangel commented: 'I would confine the period of our most effective service to the period when we were led by General Rennenkampf. From the moment that he was wounded and forced to surrender the command, our unit seemed to lose the impetuous mobility and vigorous aggression that had been so troubling to the enemy.'

Despite not being fully recovered from his wounds, Rennenkampf returned to duty in time to take part in the climactic Battle of Mukden (now Shenyang, China) between 20 February and 10 March 1905, where his conduct during the battle earned the praise of friend and foe alike. Indeed the only negative reflection on his service in the Far East would seem to be an alleged altercation with a fellow cavalry officer – Major-General Alexander Samsonov – which, although the incident is now generally regarded as a fabrication, is still often used as a 'reason' for the apparent non-cooperation of the Russian armies during the East Prussian campaign.

Humiliated on the battlefield, Russia was in need of heroes, and although he outwardly reflected the image of the swaggering, moustachioed horseman, the inwardly conscientious Rennenkampf seemed to fit the bill exactly. He left Manchuria in command of the VII Siberian Corps, and helped to suppress the 1905 Revolution, thereby gaining a reputation as a reliable and hard-working officer, one that whilst earning him the loyalty of his troops, also won him the emnity of a number of senior officers, who were resentful of his successes.

At the end of 1906, Rennenkampf returned to the West, assuming command of the III Corps at Vilnius – a position he held until January 1913, when he was appointed commander of the Vilnius Military District. With the outbreak of hostilities in the summer of 1914, it was inevitable that he be given a field command, namely that of the North-Western Front's First – or Niemen – Army.

General of Cavalry Alexander Vasilievich Samsonov (1859–1914)

Five years younger than his co-commander during the invasion of East Prussia, Samsonov entered the Vladimir Cadet School in Kiev aged 16, before transferring to the prestigious Nikolaev Cavalry School in St Petersburg. Upon graduation he was assigned to the 12th (Akhtyrsk) Hussars, and was almost immediately sent to the Balkans, where he took part in the Russo-Turkish War (1877–78).

After his service during the war, Samsonov attended the General Staff College in St Petersburg, from which he graduated in 1884. Transferred to the Caucasian Military District, he served on the staff of the 20th Infantry Division, being promoted to captain, and ultimately he became responsible for the drafting of mobilization plans for the district's Cossack regiments.

Alexander Samsonov, commander of the Russian Second Army. (Wikimedia Commons)

In March 1890, Samsonov was promoted to lieutenant-colonel and moved to the staff of the Warsaw Military District. It was here that he was seconded to the 21st (Belorussian) Dragoons, where, as interim quartermaster, he was to learn the requirements of raising and maintaining a regiment of cavalry. The experience proved invaluable when he found himself transferred once more, this time to act as superintendent of the Elysavet Cavalry Cadet School (now Kropyvnytskyi, Ukraine); during this tenure, he was promoted to major-general.

When war with Japan broke out, Samsonov was taken from his classroom and given command of the Ussurian Cossack Brigade. On 17 May 1904 – in the run-up to the Battle of Nanshan (24–26 May 1904), he led his troopers to victory over a similarly sized force of Japanese horsemen. It was an auspicious start to a battle which would ultimately be lost by the incompetence of Lieutenant-General Alexander Fok – commander of the Russian tactical reserve – who withdrew from the battlefield without informing his closest colleagues, rendering the whole Russian position untenable, and instigating a retreat in which the Russians were to lose more men than they had during the battle itself.

Samsonov led his troopers with credit during the Russian defeats at the battles of Tashihchiao and Hsimucheng (now Dashiqao and Ximucheng, China) leading to the pivotal Battle of Liaoyang, where his brigade was instrumental in keeping the Russian line of retreat open in the face of the Japanese pursuit. On 2 September, he was given command of the Siberian Cossack Division (4th, 5th and 6th regiments and 20th Horse Artillery), which he led at the battles of Shaho, Sandepu and Mukden; it was for his conduct during the course of the latter that he received his promotion to lieutenant-general.

If Rennenkampf returned from the war the moustachioed cavalier, then Samsonov was no less his bearded counterpart, being assigned as chief of staff to the Warsaw Military District. In 1907, Samsonov was appointed to command the Don Army, and on 17 March 1909 he was made governor-general of Turkestan and commander of the eponymous military district.

On 6 December 1910 – aged 51 – Samsonov became a general of cavalry. In the summer of 1914, as part of Russia's preparations for war, he transferred once more to Warsaw, where he was given command of the Second (Narew) Army in time for the invasion of East Prussia.

GERMAN

Generaloberst Maximilian Gustav Mortiz von Prittwitz und Gaffron (1848–1917)

Prittwitz began his military career as a cadet in the Prussian 3rd Guard Grenadiers, seeing service at the battles of Soor and Königgratz during the war of 1866. He received a promotion to ensign and transferred to the 38th (Silesian) Füsilier Regiment, in which regiment he served during the Franco-Prussian War. With the coming of peace in 1871, his career path or *Militärische Laufbahn* alternated regimental and staff duties, culminating with his appointment as chief of staff to IX.Armee-Korps with the rank of lieutenant-colonel.

Promotion to full colonel, and an appointment as chief of staff to the 'Northern Army' was followed by the command of first the 19. and then the 20.Infanterie-Brigade with the rank of major-general, succeeded by divisional command and promotion to lieutenant-general in 1901. Five years later, as a general of infantry, he was given command of the XVI.Armee-Korps in Metz.

In 1910, he was appointed to the Upper House of the Prussian parliament, and three years later, he received his promotion to full general or *Generaloberst* with command of the 1.Armee Inspectorate based in Danzig. As part of the German mobilization in August 1914, the three formations comprising the inspectorate (I., XVII. and XX.Armee-Korps) were allocated to the newly forming 8.Armee in East Prussia with Prittwitz assuming field command.

General der Infanterie Paul Ludwig von Beneckendorff und von Hindenburg (1847–1934)

Born into an aristocratic *Junker* (landed nobility) family in Posen, East Prussia (now Poznan, Poland) in 1847, Hindenburg first saw

Maximilian von Prittwitz und Gaffron. Out of his depth and outmanoeuvred by von François, Prittwitz was perhaps the most high-profile German 'casualty' of the Battle of Tannenberg. (Author's collection)

Paul von Beneckendorff und von Hindenburg – the 'safe pair of hands' whose management skills salveaged victory from potential defeat at Tannenberg. (Author's collection)

active service as a lieutenant with the Prussian 3rd Foot Guards in 1866 and then in the Franco-Prussian War, where he suffered a severe head wound. He recovered sufficiently to represent his regiment at the acclamation of Wilhelm I as German Kaiser in the Hall of Mirrors at Versailles.

With the war over, Hindenburg's career path would normally have settled into that of a regular peacetime officer, but in 1873 he was selected to attend the Kriegsakademie in Berlin, qualifying for service on the Greater General Staff with the rank of captain. By 1881, he was a major serving on the staff of the 1.Infanterie-Division in Königsberg, later transferring to the War Ministry in Berlin, where he led the II Department, concerned with supply and logistics, with the rank of lieutenant-colonel.

In 1896, Hindenburg was appointed chief of staff to the VIII.Armee-Korps in Koblenz, as colonel, and was promoted to major-general the following year. With the new century, Hindenburg was appointed to command the 28.Infanterie-Division with the rank of lieutenant-general. Command of IV.Armee-Korps followed in 1903, with an advancement to the rank of general of infantry two years later. At this time he was touted as one of the possible contenders to succeed Alfred von Schlieffen as Chief of the Greater General Staff, a role which ultimately went to Helmuth von Moltke (the younger).

In March 1911, Hindenburg retired from the army, in his own words 'to make way for the advancement of deserving younger officers'. But instead of retiring to his family estates in East Prussia, he took up residence at the Villa Köhler in Hanover. In August 1914, he ended his retirement at Moltke's request to assume the command of 8.Armee in East Prussia.

Generalmajor Erich Friedrich Wilhelm Ludendorff (1865–1937)

Scion of a family of minor East Prussian nobility, Ludendorff received his first commission in 1872 as a junior lieutenant in the 57th Infantry Regiment. He remained with this unit until 1887, when he transferred to the marine infantry, serving in the frigates *Niobe*, *Baden* and *Kaiser* before eventually taking the entrance exams for the Greater General Staff, in which he was appointed to the 1st – or Russian – department.

Promotion to captain came in 1895, followed by an appointment as second staff officer (I b) with IV.Armee-Korps. Two years later, Ludendorff transferred back to a company command in a line regiment, before receiving a transfer to the 9.Infanterie-Division as a major and senior staff officer. In 1902, he assumed the same role with the V.Armee-Korps.

Erich Ludendorff – the Hero of Liège. Ludendorff was Hindenburg's right-hand man, who later became a political rival. (Author's collection)

Two years later, Ludendorff returned to the Greater General Staff where, despite the regard in which he was held by his senior officers, his outspokenness won him few friends among his contemporaries. Involved with mobilization planning, he was integral to the development and continual revision of the Schlieffen Plan. Following promotions to lieutenant-colonel in 1908 and colonel in 1911, he left the general staff to assume command of Füsilier-Regiment 39, a move which Ludendorff chose to view as a deliberate attempt by his enemies to sabotage his career as a staff officer.

In April 1914, Ludendorff was promoted to *Generalmajor* and given command of the 85.Infanterie-Brigade. When war became imminent, his staff experience ensured that he was 'stepped up', being appointed Headquarters Chief of 2.Armee. On 6 August, Ludendorff was able to take advantage of the confused fighting in Liège to obtain the garrison's surrender, for which exploit he was awarded the Pour le Mérite or 'Blue Max'.

OPPOSING FORCES

RUSSIAN

Under the aegis of the North-Western Front, based in St Petersburg, two armies were called into being for the invasion of East Prussia.

The first of these, and numerically the First (or Niemen) Army, was to be commanded by General of Cavalry Paul von Rennenkampf, a decorated veteran of the Russo-Japanese War. On paper it would consist of a Guards Infantry Corps,[1] the III, IV and XX Army corps, to which were attached the 1st–3rd Cavalry divisions, and the 1st and 2nd Guards Cavalry divisions.

The Second (or Narew) Army was to be led by General of Cavalry Alexander Samsonov, likewise a decorated veteran of the war of 1904–05, under whose command would be the II, VI, XIII, XIV and XXIII Army corps, together with the 15th and 16th Cavalry divisions.

Each army corps consisted of two divisions together with an artillery brigade. Each division contained two brigades, and each brigade two regiments of infantry, each of four battalions.

A colourized contemporary photograph shown a typical Russian infantryman who fought during the Battle of Tannenberg. (Author's collection)

The corps artillery brigade was organized into two tactical divisions each of three batteries. Originally these were organized into eight-gun units, but in 1913, and in preparation for the coming conflict, the government ordered a change to more manageable six-gun batteries, which would enable a broader coverage of the available artillery support.

In total, each army corps would therefore comprise some 32 infantry battalions and between 36 and 48 guns.

In a parallel organization, the line cavalry divisions each consisted of two brigades, each of two regiments, supported by a horse artillery division organized into two batteries. The Guards divisions also consisted of two brigades, each of which would contain between two and four regiments, whilst the attached artillery divisions held three batteries each.

In terms of numbers and including all supplementary units, the First Army would consist of some 176,000 infantry, 23,000 cavalry, 408 machine guns and 696 pieces of artillery. Samsonov's Second Army would be made up of 178,000 infantry, 18,000 cavalry, 384 machine guns and 636 artillery guns. All in all, the Russians would field a force of just under 400,000 men.

1   The Guards Infantry Corps would not actually take the field with First Army, the imbalance of forces being corrected early in the campaign by the transfer of II Army Corps between the two commands.

A German field telephone section. Adequate modern communications gave the German forces a significant advantage over their Russian opponents. (Bundesarchiv, Bild 146-1970-038-68/CC-BY-SA 3.0, CC BY-SA 3.0 DE)

GERMAN

As Germany commenced its preparations for war, its forces in the East consisted of the I., II., V., VI., XVII. and XX.Armee-Korps, but in accordance with operational planning three of these would be transferred to the West leaving I.Armee-Korps (headquartered at Königsberg), XVII. Armee-Korps (Danzig) and XX.Armee-Korps (Allenstein) to form the core of 8.Armee, under the command of Generaloberst Maximilian von Prittwiz und Gaffron, hitherto commander of the 1.Armee Inspectorate at Königsberg.

Prittwitz's forces would soon be augmented by the mobilization of the I.Reserve-Korps, the 3.Reserve-Division and the 1.Kavallerie-Division, together with various second- and third-tier formations – such as replacement cadres for the line and reserve formations, the Landwehr and Landsturm, as well as the garrisons of fortresses such as Königsberg, Thorn, Graudenz and Marienburg.

With the exception of the XVII.Armee-Korps – which had been raised in Pomerania – all of these formations had been raised in East Prussia and would be fighting both figuratively and literally 'on home soil'.

In terms of sub-units, the German corps were almost identical in composition to their Russian opponents, each fielding a total of 32 infantry battalions, supported by two artillery brigades, each consisting of two artillery regiments each of two battalions. The first battalion of the senior regiment and both battalions of the junior regiment deployed three six-gun batteries of the Krupp 7.7cm field gun (FK 96). In the second battalion of the senior regiment the field guns were replaced by the Krupp version of the Rheinmetall 10.5cm field howitzer (leFH 98/09).

As part of the peacetime establishment, each infantry division had a cavalry regiment attached, but upon mobilization they were withdrawn and consolidated into a divisional-sized formation under army command.

Continuing the theme of criminality, this contemporary postcard refers to Russian arsonists being attacked by German Uhlans. (Author's collection)

ORDERS OF BATTLE

GERMAN

8.ARMEE

Generaloberst Maximilian von Prittwitz (replaced by General der Infanterie Paul von Hindenburg)

I.Armee-Korps (Field HQ – Generalleutnant Hermann von François)
Füßartillerie-Regiment 1, Bataillon 1 (heavy field howitzers)
1.Infanterie-Division (Generalleutnant Richard von Conta)
1.Brigade
  Grenadier-Regiment 1 (Crown Prince – 1st East Prussian)
  Infanterie-Regiment 41 (von Boyen – 5th East Prussian)
2.Brigade
  Grenadier-Regiment 3 (King Friedrich Wilhelm I – 2nd East Prussian)
  Infanterie-Regiment 43 (Duke Karl of Mecklenburg – 6th East Prussian)
Ulanen-Regiment 8 (Count Dohna – 8th East Prussian)
1.Feldartillerie-Brigade
  Feldartillerie-Regiment 16 (1st East Prussian)
  Feldartillerie-Regiment 52 (2nd East Prussian)
2.Infanterie-Division (Generalleutnant Adalbert von Falk)
3.Brigade
  Grenadier-Regiment 4 (King Friedrich II – 3rd East Prussian)
  Infanterie-Regiment 44 (Count Döhnhoff – 7th East Prussian)
4.Brigade
  Füsilier-Regiment 33 (Count Roon – 4th East Prussian)
  Infanterie-Regiment 45 (8th East Prussian)
Jäger-Regiment zu Pferde 10
2.Feldartillerie-Brigade
  Feldartillerie-Regiment 1 (Prince August of Prussia – 1st Lithuanian)
  Feldartillerie-Regiment 37 (2nd Lithuanian)

XVII.Armee-Korps (General der Kavallerie August von Mackensen)
Füßartillerie-Regiment 11 (1st West Prussian), Bataillon 1 (heavy field howitzers)
35.Infanterie-Division (Generalleutnant Otto Hennig)
70.Brigade
  Infanterie-Regiment 21 (Von Borcke – 4th Pomeranian)
  Infanterie-Regiment 61 (Von der Marwitz – 8th Pomeranian)
87.Brigade
  Infanterie-Regiment 141 (Kulm)
  Infanterie-Regiment 176 (9th West Prussian)
  Jäger Battalion 2 (Prince von Bismarck – Pomeranian)

Jäger-Regiment zu Pferde 4
Feldartillerie-Brigade 35
  Feldartillerie-Regiment 71 (Großkomtur)
  Feldartillerie-Regiment 81 (Thorn), Bataillon 1
36.Infanterie-Division (Generalleutnant der Artillerie Konstanz von Heineccius)
69.Infanterie-Brigade
  Infanterie-Regiment 129 (3rd West Prussian)
  Infanterie-Regiment 175 (8th West Prussian)
71.Infanterie-Brigade
  Grenadier Regiment 5 (King Friedrich I – 4th East Prussian)
  Infanterie-Regiment 128 (Danzig)
Husaren-Regiment 5 (Prince Blücher von Wahlstatt – Pomeranian)
36.Feldartillerie-Brigade
  Feldartillerie-Regiment 36 (2nd West Prussian), Bataillon 1
  Feldartillerie-Regiment 72 (Hochmeister)

XX.Armee-Korps (General der Artillerie Friedrich von Scholtz)
II./Füßartillerie-Regiment 5 (heavy field howitzers)
37.Infanterie-Division (Generalleutnant Hermann von Staabs)
73.Infanterie-Brigade
  Infanterie-Regiment 147 (2nd Masurian)
  Infanterie-Regiment 151 (2nd Ermländ)
  Jäger Battalion 1 (Graf Yorck von Wartenburg – East Prussian)
75.Infanterie-Brigade
  Infanterie-Regiment 146 (1st Masurian)
  Infanterie-Regiment 150 (1st Ermländ)
37.Feldartillerie-Brigade
  Feldartillerie-Regiment 73 (1st Masurian)
  Feldartillerie-Regiment 82 (2nd Masurian)
Dragoner-Regiment 11 (von Wedel – Pomeranian)
41.Infanterie-Division (Generalmajor Leo Sontag)
72.Infanterie-Brigade
  Infanterie-Regiment 18 (Von Grollmann – 1st Posen)
  Infanterie-Regiment 59 (Freiherr Hiller von Gärtringen – 4th Posen)
74.Infanterie-Brigade
  Infanterie-Regiment 148 (5th West Prussian)
  Infanterie-Regiment 152 (Deutscher Orden)
Dragoner-Regiment 10 (King Albert von Sachsen – East Prussian)
41.Feldartillerie-Brigade
  Feldartillerie-Regiment 35 (1st West Prussian)
  Feldartillerie-Regiment 79 (3rd East Prussian)
1.Kavallerie-Division (Generalleutnant Hermann Brecht)

1.Kavallerie-Brigade
  Kürassier-Regiment 3 (Count Wrangel – East Prussian)
  Dragoner-Regiment 1 (Prince Albrecht of Prussia – Lithuanian)
2.Kavallerie-Brigade
  Ulanen-Regiment 12 (Lithuanian)
  Jäger-Regiment zu Pferde 9
41.Kavallerie-Brigade
  Kürassier-Regiment 5 (Duke Friedrich Eugen von Württemberg – West Prussian)
  Ulanen-Regiment 4 (Von Schmidt – 1st Pomeranian)
Feldartillerie-Regiment 1 (Horse Artillery Detachment – Prince August of Prussia – 1st Lithuanian)

I.Reserve-Korps (Generalleutnant Otto von Below)
1.Reserve-Division (Generalleutant Arthur von Förster)
1.Reserve-Infanterie-Brigade
  Reserve-Infanterie-Regiment 1
  Reserve-Infanterie-Regiment 3
72.Reserve-Infanterie-Brigade
  Reserve-Infanterie-Regiment 18
  Reserve-Infanterie-Regiment 59
  Reserve-Jäger-Bataillon 1
Reserve-Ulanen-Regiment 1
Reserve-Feldartillerie-Regiment 1
36.Reserve-Division (Generalleutnant Curt Kruge)
69.Reserve-Infanterie-Brigade
  Reserve-Infanterie-Regiment 21
  Reserve-Infanterie-Regiment 61
  Reserve-Jäger Bataillon 2
70.Reserve-Infanterie-Brigade
  Reserve-Infanterie-Regiment 5
  Reserve-Infanterie-Regiment 54
Reserve-Husaren-Regiment 1
Reserve-Feldartillerie-Regiment 36
3.Reserve-Division (Generalleutnant Kurt von Morgen)
5.Reserve-Infanterie-Brigade
  Reserve-Infanterie-Regiment 2
  Reserve-Infanterie-Regiment 9
6.Reserve-Infanterie-Brigade
  Reserve-Infanterie-Regiment 34
  Reserve-Infanterie-Regiment 49
Reserve-Dragoner-Regiment 5
Reserve-Feldartillerie-Regiment 3
Composite Infanterie-Division (Generalmajor Fritz von Unger)
20.Landwehr-Brigade
  Landwehr-Infanterie-Regiment 19
  Landwehr-Infanterie-Regiment 107
  Reserve-Schwere-Kavallerie-Regiment 3 (less 2nd and 3rd squadrons)
Ersatz-Brigade 'von Semmern'[2]
  Ersatz-Infanterie bataillonen 5, 59, 129, 141 and 175
  Ersatz-Feldartillerie-Regiment 72
  Ersatz-Feldartillerie-Regiment 73, 1.Batterie

2   *Ersatz* indicates a replacement unit.

Höherer Landwehr Kommandeur 1
(Generalleutnant Georg Freiherr von
der Goltz)
33.Landwehr-Brigade
Landwehr-Infanterie-Regiment 75
Landwehr-Infanterie-Regiment 76
34.Landwehr-Brigade
Landwehr-Infanterie-Regiment 31
Landwehr-Infanterie-Regiment 84
Landwehr-Feldartillerie (ex-IX.Armee-Korps),
1. and 2.Batterie
Reserve-Fußartillerie-Regiment 17, 2. and
4.Batterie

5.Landwehr-Infanterie-Brigade
(Generalleutnant Friedrich von
Mülmann)
Landwehr-Infanterie-Regiment 2
Landwehr-Infanterie-Regiment 9
Ersatz-Feldartillerie-Regiment 1, 1.Batterie
Reserve-Fußartillerie-Regiment 11, 1.Bataillon
Reserve-Füßartillerie-Regiment 15, 4.Batterie
6.Landwehr-Infanterie-Brigade
(Generalmajor Adolf Krahmer)
Landwehr-Infanterie-Regiment 34
Landwehr-Infanterie-Regiment 49
Landwehr-Kavallerie-Regiment (ex-Garde/

IX.Armee-Korps)
Landsturm-Feldartillerie-Regiment
(ex-II.Armee-Korps), 1. and 2.Batterie
70.Landwehr-Infanterie-Brigade
(Generalmajor Adolf Breithaupt)
Landwehr-Infanterie-Regiment 5
Landwehr-Infanterie-Regiment 18
Landwehr-Kavallerie-Regiment (ex-XVII.
Armee-Korps) – two squadrons
Landwehr-Kavallerie-Regiment
(ex-XX.Armee-Korps)
Landsturm-Feldartillerie-Regiment
(ex-XVII.Armee-Korps), 1. and 2.Batterie

RUSSIAN

RUSSIAN FIRST ARMY

General of Cavalry Paul von Rennenkampf

**II Army Corps (General of Cavalry Sergei
Mikhailovich Scheidemann)**
**26th Infantry Division (Lieutenant-
General Alexander Poretsky)**
1st Brigade
101st Infantry Regiment (Perm)
102nd Infantry Regiment (Vyatka)
2nd Brigade
103rd Infantry Regiment (Pedrozavodsk)
104th Infantry Regiment (Ustyug –
General Prince Bagration's)
26th Artillery Brigade
**43rd Infantry Division (Lieutenant-
General Vladimir Alekseevich
Slyusarenko)**
1st Brigade
169th Infantry Regiment (Novo Troksk)
170th Infantry Regiment (Molodechno)
2nd Brigade
171st Infantry Regiment (Kobrin)
172nd Infantry Regiment (Lida)
43rd Artillery Brigade
**2nd Cavalry Division (Lieutenant-
General Hussein, Khan
Nakhichevansky)**
1st Brigade
2nd Leib Dragoner Regiment (Pskov –
HIM[3] Tsarina Maria Feodorovna's)
2nd Leib Ulanen Regiment (Courland –
HIM Tsar Alexander III's)
2nd Brigade
2nd Leib Husaren Regiment (Pavlograd
– HIM Tsar Nicholas II's)
2nd Don Cossack Regiment (HIM
Tsarevich Alexei Nikolaevich's)
2nd Horse Artillery Division
2nd Howitzer Artillery Division

**III Army Corps (General of Infantry
Nikolai Aleksevich Yepanchin)**
**25th Infantry Division (Lieutenant-
General Pavel Ilyich Bulgakov)**
1st Brigade
97th Infantry Regiment (Livonia – Field
Marshal Count Sheremetev's)
98th Infantry Regiment (Vyatka)

2nd Brigade
103rd Infantry Regiment (Pedrozavodsk)
104th Infantry Regiment (Ustyug –
General Prince Bagration's)
25th Artillery Brigade
**27th Infantry Division
(Lieutenant-General August Karl
Mikhail Mikhailovich Adaridi)**
1st Brigade
105th Infantry Regiment (Orenburg)
106th Infantry Regiment (Ufa)
2nd Brigade
107th Infantry Regiment (Troitski –
'Holy Trinity')
108th Infantry Regiment (Saratov)
27th Artillery Brigade
**3rd Cavalry Division (Lieutenant-General
Vladimir Karlovich Belgard)**
1st Brigade
3rd Dragoon Regiment (Novorossiysk
– HIM The Grand Duchess Elena
Vladimirovna's)
3rd Ulan Regiment (Smolensk – HIM
The Tsar Alexander III's)
2nd Brigade
3rd Hussar Regiment (Elisavetgrad)
3rd Don Cossack Regiment (Yermak
Timofeevich's)
3rd Horse Artillery Division
**5th Independent Rifle Brigade
(Major-General Petr Dmitrievich
Shreider)**
17th Rifle Regiment
18th Rifle Regiment
19th Rifle Regiment
20th Rifle Regiment
5th Rifle Artillery Division
3rd Howitzer Artillery Division

**IV Army Corps (General of Artillery Eris-
Khan Sultan-Giray Aliyev)**
**30th Infantry Division (Lieutenant-
General Eduard Arkadevich
Kolyanovsky)**
1st Brigade
117th Infantry Regiment (Yaroslalvl)
118th Infantry Regiment (Shuya)
2nd Brigade
119th Infantry Regiment (Kolomna)
120th Infantry Regiment (Serpukhov)
30th Artillery Brigade
**40th Infantry Division (Lieutenant-
General Nikolai Nikolaevich
Korotkevich)**

1st Brigade
157th Infantry Regiment (Imeretia)
158th Infantry Regiment (Kutais)
2nd Brigade
159th Infantry Regiment (Guria)
160th Infantry Regiment (Abkhazia)
40th Artillery Brigade
4th Howitzer Artillery Battalion

**XX Army Corps (General of Infantry
Vladimir Vasilievich Smirnov)**
**28th Infantry Division (Lieutenant-
General Nikolai Alekseevich
Lashkevich)**
1st Brigade
109th Infantry Regiment (Volga)
110th Infantry Regiment (Kama)
2nd Brigade
111th Infantry Regiment (Don)
112th Infantry Regiment (Ural)
28th Artillery Brigade
**29th Infantry Division (Lieutenant-
General Anatoly Nikolaevich
Rosenschild von Paulin)**
1st Brigade
113th Infantry Regiment (Staraya Russia)
114th Infantry Regiment (Novye-Torzhok)
2nd Brigade
115th Infantry Regiment (Vyazma)
116th Infantry Regiment
(Maloyaroslavets)
29th Artillery Brigade
**1st Independent Cavalry Brigade
(Major-General Nikolai Aloizievich
Oranovsky)**
19th Dragoon Regiment (Archangel)
16th Hussar Regiment (Irkutsk)
20th Howitzer Artillery Battalion
1st Heavy Artillery Battalion
**1st Guard Cavalry Division (Lieutenant-
General Nikolai Nikolaievich
Kaznakov)**
1st Brigade
Chevalier Garde Regiment (HIM Tsarina
Maria Theodorovna's)
Leibgarde zu Pferd Regiment
2nd Brigade
Leibgarde Kürassier Regiment (HIM Tsar
Nicholas II's)
Leibgarde Kürassier Regiment (HIM
Tsarina Maria Theodorovna's)
3rd Brigade
Leib Don Cossack Regiment (HIM Tsar
Nicholas II's)
Leib Ataman Cossack Regiment (HIH

3 In the list that follows, HIM refers to His/Her Imperial
Majesty; HIH to His/Her Imperial Highness; HRH to
His/Her Royal Highness; and HM to His/Her
Majesty).

Tsarevich Alexei Nicolaevich's)
Leib Composite Cossack Regiment
Life Guards Horse Artillery Brigade,
1st Division

2nd Guards Cavalry Division (Lieutenant-General Georgi Ottonovich Rauch)
1st Brigade
Leibgarde Grenadier Regiment zu Pferd
Leibgarde Ulanen Regiment (HIM Tsarina Maria Theodorovna's)
2nd Brigade
Leibgarde Dragoner Regiment
Leibgarde Husaren Regiment (HIM Tsar Nicholas II's)
Life Guards Horse Artillery Brigade,
2nd Division

1st Cavalry Division (Lieutenant-General Vasily Iosifovich Romeiko-Gurko)
1st Brigade
1st Leib Ulanen Regiment (Moscow – HIM Tsar Peter I's)
1st Ulanen Regiment (St Petersburg – Field Marshal Prince Menshikov's)
2nd Brigade
1st Hussar Regiment (Sumy – General Alexander Seslavin's)
1st Don Cossack Regiment (Generalissimo Alexander, Prince Suvorov's)
1st Horse Artillery Division

RUSSIAN SECOND ARMY

General of Cavalry Alexander Vasilievich Samsonov

I Army Corps (General of Infanry Leonid Konstantinovich Artmanov)
22nd Infantry Division (Lieutenant-General Sergei Dmitrievich Markov)
1st Brigade
85th Infantry Regiment (HIM Kaiser Wilhelm II's Viborg)
86th Infantry Regiment (Villmanstrand)
2nd Brigade
87th Infantry Regiment (Nyslott)
88th Infantry Regiment (Petrovsk)
22nd Artillery Brigade
24th Infantry Division (Lieutenant-General Nikolai Petrovich Reschikov)
1st Brigade
93rd Infantry Regiment (Grand Duke Michael's Irkutsk)
94th Infantry Regiment (Yeniseisk)
2nd Brigade
95th Infantry Regiment (Krasnoyarsk)
96th Infantry Regiment (Omsk)
24th Artillery Brigade
1st Howitzer Artillery Battalion

VI Army Corps (General of Infantry Alexander Alexandrovich Blagoveschensky)
4th Infantry Division (Lieutenant-General Nikolai Nikolaievich Komarov)
1st Brigade
13th Infantry Regiment (Belozersk – Field Marshal Prince Volkonsky's)
14th Infantry Regiment (Olonets – HM King Peter I of Serbia's)
2nd Brigade
15th Infantry Regiment (Schlüsselburg

– General Field Marshal the Prince Anikita Repnin's)
16th Infantry Regiment (Ladoga)
4th Artillery Brigade
16th Infantry Division (Lieutenant-General Guido Kazimirovich Richter)
1st Brigade
61st Infantry Regiment (Vladimir)
62nd Infantry Regiment (Suzdal Generalissimo Prince Suvorov's)
2nd Brigade
63rd Infantry Regiment (Uglich – General Field Marshal Apraksin's)
64th Infantry Regiment (Kazan)
16th Artillery Brigade
4th Cavalry Division (Lieutenant-General Anton Alexandrovich Tolpygo)
1st Brigade
4th Dragoon Regiment (Novotroitsk-Yekaterinoslav – Field Marshal Prince Potemkin-Tauride's)
4th Ulan Regiment (Kharkov)
2nd Brigade
4th Hussar Regiment (Mariupol – General Field Marshal Prince Wittgenstein's)
4th Don Cossack Regiment (Count Platov's)
4th Horse Artillery Division (Colonel Vladimir Koronatovich Latukhin)
6th Howitzer Artillery Battalion

XIII Army Corps (Lieutenant-General Nikolai Alekseevich Klujew)
1st Infantry Division (Lieutenant-General Andrei Alexandrovich Ugryumov)
1st Brigade
1st Infantry Regiment (Neva – HM The King of the Hellenes')
2nd Infantry Regiment (Sofia – HIM Tsar Alexander III's)
2nd Brigade
3rd Infantry Regiment (Narva – General Field Marshal Prince Michael Golitzyn's)
4th Infantry Regiment (Korpore – General Pyotr Petrovich, Count Konovitsyn's)
1st Artillery Brigade
36th Infantry Division (Lieutenant-General Alexander Bogdanovich Prezhentsov)
1st Brigade
141st Infantry Regiment (Mozhaisk)
142nd Infantry Regiment (Zvenigorod)
2nd Brigade
143rd infantry Regiment (Dorogobuzh)
144th Infantry Regiment (Kashira)
36th Artillery Brigade
2nd Independent Cavalry Brigade (Lieutenant-General Abram Mikhailovich Dragomirov)
17th Hussar Regiment (Chernigov – HIH Grand Duke Michael Alexandrovich's)
18th Hussar Regiment (Nezhin)
Replacement Horse Artillery Division
13th Howitzer Artillery Battalion
5th Heavy Artillery Battalion

XV Army Corps (General of Infantry Nikolai Nikolaievich Martos)
6th Infantry Division (Lieutenant-General Fedor Ivanovich Torklus)
1st Brigade
21st Infantry Regiment (Murom)
22nd Infantry Regiment (Nishnii-Novgorod – HIH the Grand Duchess Vera Konstantinova's)
2nd Brigade
23rd Infantry Regiment (Nizovskii – Field Marshal Ivan, Count Saltykov's)
24th Infantry Regiment (Simbirsk – General Dmitri General Neverovsky's)
6th Artillery Brigade
8th Infantry Division (Lieutenant-General Yevgeny Emilievich, Baron Fitinghof)
1st Brigade
29th Infantry Regiment (Chernigov – Field Marshal Count Diebitsch-Zabalkansky's)
30th Infantry Regiment (Poltava)
2nd Brigade
31st Infantry Regiment (Aleksopol)
32nd Infantry Regiment (Kremenchug)
8th Artillery Brigade
15th Howitzer Artillery Battalion

XXIII Army Corps (General of Infantry Kyprian Antonovich Kondratovich)
2nd Infantry Division (Lieutenant-General Alexander Alexandrovich Dushkevich)
1st Brigade
5th Infantry Regiment (Kaluga – HIM Kaiser Wilhelm I's)
6th Infantry Regiment (Libau – HRH Prince Friedrich-Leopold of Prussia's)
2nd Brigade
7th Infantry Regiment (Reval – General Schuchov's)
8th Infantry Regiment (Estonia)
2nd Artillery Brigade
(The remainder of XXIII Army Corps was still in the process of assembling and moving up to the front line at the time of the Battle of Tannenberg.)
6th Cavalry Division (Lieutenant-General Vladimir Khristoforovich Roop)
1st Brigade
6th Dragoon Regiment (Glukhov – HIM Tsarina Catherine II's)
6th Ulan Regiment (Volhynia)
2nd Brigade
6th Hussar Regiment (Klyastitsky – HRH Grand Duke Ernst-Ludwig of Hesse's)
6th Don Cossack Regiment (Ataman Ivan Mateevich Krasnoshchekov's)
6th Horse Artillery Division
15th Cavalry Division (Lieutenant-General Pavel Petrovich Lyubomirov)
1st Brigade
15th Dragoon Regiment (Pereyaslav – HIM Tsar Alexander III's)
15th Ulan Regiment (Tatar)
2nd Brigade
15th Hussar Regiment (Ukraine – HIH Grand Duchess Ksenia Alexandrovna's)
3rd Ural Cossack Regiment
15th Horse Artillery Division

OPPOSING PLANS

RUSSIAN

From the outset, and given that its estimates of the German forces defending East Prussia would be no more than four army corps, supported by reserve and second-tier formations, Russia planned to concentrate its forces close to the border. The reason for this was to capitalize on the benefit of superior numbers and to open up the desired 'second front' at the earliest possible opportunity, an aspiration that was buoyed by reports that stocks of munitions and *matériel* were increasing to the levels required for offensive operations. Accordingly, the planners at Stavka – the Russian High Command – decided that a force of two full armies, containing a total of nine or ten corps plus supporting elements, would be more than sufficient to secure victory.

General Cyprian Kondratovich, commander of the Russian XXIII Corps, Second Army. (Wikimedia Commons)

The plan was that the first of these, drawn from the Vilna Military District and under the command of Paul von Rennenkampf, would invade German territory by bypassing the Masurian Lakes at their northern end before moving against the enemy's perceived left flank. The second army, mustering around the Warsaw area, would be commanded by Alexander Samsonov and, in a mirror operation, would move south of the lakes and then against the German right flank. Once they were beyond the lakes, both armies would act in concert to bring the German forces to battle and defeat them in a double envelopment.

In April 1914, and with all of the participants – with the exception of Samsonov – occupying their wartime roles, the General Staff conducted an operational wargame in Kiev to show the likely outcome of the existing War Plan. With a hypothetical German attack being beaten off and then followed up by a Russian invasion of East Prussia, the exercise was naturally a success, albeit a heavily flawed one. The reason was that, unlike the simulations that the Germans

Deployments at the outbreak of hostilities, August 1914

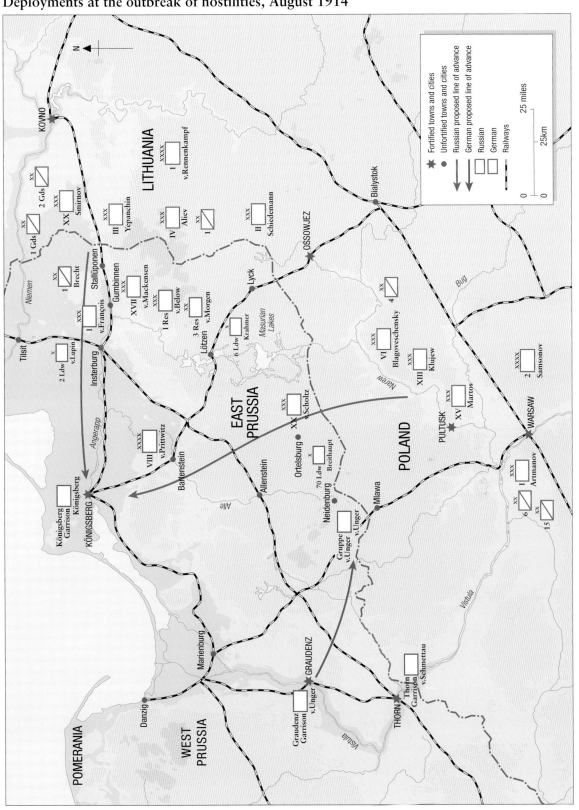

had undertaken in the previous decade, the focus of the Russian wargame had been on the deployment of the combat elements per the mobilization timetable; the whole logistical aspect had been purposely ignored in order to streamline things.

In effect, the Russian army was preparing to go to war with only the vaguest idea as to how it would maintain its forces in the field once contact had been made with the enemy. This was to ultimately prove to be the Achilles heel in Stavka's planning.

In addition, there was a further consideration that would prove to have an influence on the Russian deployment. Just like relations between Austria-Hungary and Serbia, both Poland and Lithuania had only been integrated into Russia a century or so earlier, and both contained nationalist elements that agitated against its rule. As a result of these tensions, a sufficient military presence was needed to maintain the rearward lines of communication between the armies in the field and their depots.

GERMAN

Presented by Field Marshal Alfred von Schlieffen shortly before his retirement in early 1906, the core principle of what has become known as the Schlieffen Plan was to provide a viable strategy which would prevent Germany from being embroiled in a lengthy two-front war. It should be stressed that, contrary to common opinion, it was not specifically the blueprint for a German invasion of France.

The confusion arises from the fact that when Schlieffen made his original submission in late 1905, Russia was deemed to have been so weakened by its experiences during the Russo-Japanese War (1904–05) that a two-front war was – to the general staff – unimaginable. This assumption changed when Schlieffen was replaced by Generaloberst Helmuth von Moltke, whose opinion – rationally enough – was that Russia's tribulations would not last forever, and that in any future variations of the plan its full participation needed to be considered.

Oberstleutnant Carl Maximilian Hoffmann, arguably the man behind the development of the German plan of battle. (Bundesarchiv, Bild 146-2008-0278/CC-BY-SA 3.0, CC BY-SA 3.0 DE)

In principle the plan called for the massing of German resources against one of its potential enemies in order to secure a favourable strategic result, whilst on the other – weaker – front its regular forces, bolstered by second- and third-tier formations, together with local garrisons, would conduct what is described as an 'active defence' until reinforced and relieved.

In the event, the Oberste Heeresleitung (OHL – Supreme Army Command) decided to adopt the second variant – or *Aufmarsch II* – of the plan, which indeed saw France as the primary target. As the troops were deployed in the West, it fell to Prittwitz, in command of 8.Armee, to devise a strategy for the defence of East Prussia.

Like their enemy, the members of the German General Staff had conducted a number of exercises simulating a Russian invasion of East Prussia, and like their opponents the results of the German wargames had all resulted in victories for the defending forces. Unlike the Kiev session, the German ones were heavily weighted towards logistical matters, ranging from the movement of troops via the road and rail network, to the transport of military supplies and beyond, to include the transfer of intelligence and information in all its forms, whether coded or in clear, whether by radio, telegraph or telephone. In addition, special attention was given to aerial reconnaissance using both aircraft and airships.

The result of this practical planning was the concept of the 'active defence', which in effect meant that even when on the defensive, German commanders in the East would be expected to act aggressively, seizing the initiative and using it to contain the enemy in one sector whilst massing their forces in another – one where the German forces would have a chance of victory.

Without a sense of definition so beloved of the German officer corps, the concept could be described as a 'poisoned chalice', as it remained with OHL to decide whether or not the commander had been as 'active' in the execution of his duties as the plan had warranted.

THE CAMPAIGN

DER RUSSENEINFALL – RUSSIA ATTACKS

With its declaration of war against Russia on 1 August 1914 and Russia's subsequent formal mobilization, Germany found itself in a state of extreme pressure. The established plan for a war on two fronts required that one of the two potential enemies be eliminated before forces were redeployed to counter the other, but for this to happen two conditions needed to be successfully fulfilled. Firstly, that the initial attacks would be quickly and favourably resolved, and secondly, that the remaining German forces would be able to mount a successful defence until such time as the planned reinforcement had taken place and they could take the offensive.

With the Großer Generalstab (Greater General Staff) anticipating that the Russians would only be in a position to take the field some 15 days after mobilization, roughly 16–17 August, the OHL believed that Germany would have a more than sufficient window of opportunity to defeat France before turning its attention eastwards.

Despite a decade of planning and amendment, the plan almost fell at the first hurdle. Having issued a declaration of war against France on 3 August, Germany boldly demanded that Belgium grant passage for its troops. Supported by assurances from Great Britain, Brussels refused the German demands, and the following day Germany declared war upon Belgium, an announcement that was followed by a reciprocal declaration from London.

Instead of facing a war with two enemies, Berlin now found itself at war with a total of four. Despite this unexpected escalation, things initially went well for the attacking armies when, on 7 August, the Maas-Armee (Army of the Meuse) – an ad hoc formation comprising six reinforced infantry brigades and three cavalry divisions – took the Belgian city of Liège by a *coup de main*. Theoretically, this opened a land corridor wide enough to facilitate the further movement of German troops, the OHL anticipating that an advance towards the French border would take place shortly thereafter. In the event, the planned advance would be delayed by the need to reduce the belt of fortresses around the city that still remained in enemy hands.

The news of the German victory, as soon as it was received in Paris, was greeted with dread. Earlier

Der Russeneinfall – a cossack patrol is shown here together with Russian infantry. (Author's collection)

assurances had been that Russian forces would be in the field on M+15, which itself was still a week away, and as the armies still had to mass and assemble sufficient supplies to support offensive operations, it could even be a further two or even three weeks before the Tsar's troops crossed swords with the enemy. Urgent telegrams were sent to both Théophile Delcassé, the French Ambassador to St Petersburg, and to Stavka – the former being urged to use his connections at the imperial court in support of his country's interests, the latter to increase the speed of mobilization and the opening of a second front before a decision could be reached in the West.

German troops being transported by rail. The ability to use interior lines and transport infrastructure would be a significant advantage for 8.Armee. (Bundesarchiv, Bild 104-0332/CC-BY-SA 3.0/CC-BY-SA 3.0, CC BY-SA 3.0 DE)

Three days after the fall of Liège, Stavka made its announcement: the Russian advance would begin after a further three days, on 13 August. The next day, Rennenkampf's troops crossed the border into East Prussia, an event which – given the levels of destruction and atrocities that the invading forces were immediately reported to have perpetrated – became known to the Germans as *Der Russeneinfall*, with its connotations of criminal assault and damage. It would later prove to be a useful method of inciting the local population against the invader, the opposite side of the coin being the large numbers of refugees who fled the Russian advance, blocking the roads as German troops marched eastwards.

The Russian Niemen Army crossed into German territory in line abreast, with III Corps (Yepanchin) in the centre, flanked to the left and right by the parallel columns of IV Corps (Aliev) and XX Corps (Smirnov) to its left and right respectively. Almost immediately, the Russians began to feel the inadequacy of their logistical provisions – for even in the event of a suitable railhead being captured or established on enemy soil, and despite the improvements that they had made to their own railway network, the simple fact was that German and Russian railways worked on different gauges. Even if sufficient rolling stock could be assembled, supplies would still need to be transhipped from one set of wagons to another before they could be moved up to the front line.

To the south, as the Russian Second Army was also preparing to advance, its commander received a charge of orders from North-Western Front's headquarters at St Petersburg. Initially, the plan had been for Samsonov's forces to move around the southern approaches to the Masurian Lakes, and then for half of the army to cooperate with Rennenkampf's troops moving down from the north and engage the enemy's main body in a battle of encirclement; meanwhile, the remainder of his troops could either act as a blocking force to prevent other German forces from attempting to intervene, or alternately make their own drive to cut across the enemy lines of communication to split the German forces in two. But now, and in pursuit of a greater prize, Zhilinski, to whom both army commanders reported – and having been prompted by his own superiors – ordered Samsonov to realign his axis of advance in order to take him closer towards the Vistula River.

Of his original command, only the II Corps (Scheidemann) would remain in its original position, its purpose now being to act as a hinge between the two armies, whilst Samsonov moved in compliance with his new orders.

General Nikolai Martos, commander of the Russian XV Corps, Second Army. (Wikimedia Commons)

Ultimately, Scheidemann's corps would be transferred to the First Army's area of operations.

By intervening with these new orders, Zhilinski had forced a radical change in Second Army's operational timetable, but on 16 August Samsonov made an even more dramatic change by issuing orders that would extend his line of advance some 20–30 miles further westwards, his troops initially marching in a north-westerly direction before swinging northwards in order to comply with Zhilinski's instructions.

As it advanced, the main body of the Second Army was occupied by XV Corps (Martos), XIII Corps (Klujew) and finally VI Corps (Blagoveschensky), supported by the 2nd Infantry Division of XXIII Corps (Kondratovich), whose 3rd Guards Division was still forming up to the rear. In addition, I Corps (Artmanov) was released from duty in the rear in order to move up and cover the left flank of Martos' corps.

When challenged on these new orders, Samsonov responded by telling Zhilinski that he had set these new lines of advance so that his troops would have sufficient room to manoeuvre, thus having the opportunity of enveloping the enemy rather than having to engage him frontally in a slogging match with an uncertain outcome. Whether or not this was indeed the rationale behind the change is, given Samsonov's later death, uncertain, but what is certain is that at a time when both Russian armies should have been operating closely with each other, in both tactical and geographical terms, they would actually be moving apart – thus compromising any likelihood of joint action.

Having said that, it would still have been theoretically possible for Samsonov to recoup much of the time lost through these latter changes, whilst still meeting his new objectives. In order to achieve this, what would be required were days of hard marching in the excessive summer heat, across loamy terrain that he was already decrying as being impossible for his men to march upon. Moreover, all of this was to be achieved by men who until recently had been reservists and were now being thrown directly into the maelstrom of war.

What should also be stressed is that, as opposing armies manoeuvred to the inevitable moment of first contact, they remained in a grey area, one that was theoretical rather than practical, one whose fog would only be dispelled when the first shots were fired. Whilst a number of senior Russian officers had seen action in the Far East a decade earlier, the brigades and regiments that they commanded had last seen action against Turkey in 1878. For the German forces, their last action would have been the Franco-Prussian War of 1870–71, when even the oldest of those currently under arms in East Prussia would have been amongst the youngest of recruits or the most junior of junior officers.

INVASION

In the days following the German mobilization, Prittwitz deployed his forces for the campaign ahead. From its headquarters at Königsberg, the East Prussians of François' I.Armee-Korps moved east from the provincial capital to occupy positions around Gümbinnen and Insterburg, whilst the other local formation

A German infantry patrol taking cover in ruined buildings whilst observing the activity of Russian troops. (Author's collection)

– Scholtz's XX.Armee-Korps – took station to cover the southern border. From Danzig, the Pomeranians of XVII.Armee-Korps moved by rail to a new position around Soldau. Elsewhere, I.Reserve-Korps was placed around Nordenburg and Angerburg to provide direct support for François, whilst the newly constituted 1.Kavallerie-Division took station covering the lines of communication to Königsberg. The 3.Reserve-Division was sent to the fortress at Thorn, whilst – finally – the Landwehr and Landsturm units began mustering for service. It was not a perfect deployment, but given the length of the Russo-German border, and the fact that 8.Armee would inevitably be outnumbered by its Russian opponents, the army commander had to cover several eventualities simultaneously. The mist that he was confronted with would only clear when the enemy had made his move, and from then on it would be a case of divining his intentions and countering them. But for this mist to clear, Prittwitz needed accurate information regarding the enemy's concentrations and subsequent movements, and so he gave orders for his commanders to begin working on this task.

The ruins of Neidenburg, destroyed during the fighting of 22 August 1914. (Author's collection)

Under army command, Luftschiffer-Bataillon 5 based at Graudenz – deploying an airship and its attendant supports in hangars at Königsberg, Graudenz and Schneidemühl – would be invaluable in gathering the information required, as it possessed an endurance and operational range far greater than any other element at Prittwitz's disposal. However, the machines were prone to mechanical failure and their usage was not as great as it could have been. Once hostilities began, the three vessels were moved to Allenstein, Liegnitz and Posen respectively.

In addition, the German commander had the services of two companies of Flieger-Bataillon 2 based in the fortresses of Königsberg and Graudenz, the unit providing detachments or *Feldfliegerabteilungen* (FFA) of six aircraft at both army and corps level together with *Festungsfliegerabteilungen* (FestA) of four aircraft in support of the principal fortress garrisons.

Although reconnaissance flights began almost immediately, there was no real pattern to them. In the euphoria of what many believed would be a very short conflict, the aircrews were no doubt more interested in testing the capabilities of their machines rather than providing any concrete evidence as to enemy activity. But within a few days, this attitude diminished when the army staff assigned each detachment a fixed area of operations with daily reports to be submitted, evaluated and then followed up, as deemed necessary.

The first success came when pilots of FFA 14 – operating in support of I.Armee-Korps – overflew a number of marching columns, wagon parks and encampments, around Suwalki (now Suwalken, Poland). These were most likely elements of the Russian II Corps moving towards the Masurian Lakes in order to keep pace with Rennenkampf's First Army.

Feeling vindicated in his initial deployments, Prittwitz now ordered the airship *Z-IV* under Captain von Quast to conduct a further sweep towards the Polish town of Mlawa in order to confirm the lack of any enemy build-up in the area. When Quast reported that he had seen no enemy forces whatsoever, Prittwitz made the fateful decision to mass the bulk of his forces in the north to counter Rennenkampf before redeploying the troops to move against any threat which had developed in the south. With XX.Armee-Korps remaining in position, reinforced by garrison troops as well as Landwehr and Landsturm units, the rest of 8.Armee's field units were ordered to move up to the Angerapp River, their commander confident in the belief of an imminent German victory – but it was a confidence that would soon be dispelled.

Although telegraphy had been available at the time when he had last seen active service, Prittwitz had been part of an army where messages had principally been delivered either verbally or by hand, or field intelligence gathered by the naked eye. Now, four decades on, technology had caught up with and surpassed the practices of the 19th century, effectively bombarding 8.Armee with a plethora of new and constantly changing information which meant that orders given could become redundant before they had even reached their intended recipients. As the German columns moved northwards, the various *Fliegerabteilungen* began to report ever-increasing visual contacts with enemy forces.

It was an excess of information that threatened to overwhelm the army commander – his staff could analyse and evaluate reports, but ultimately their essence would need to be pushed up the chain of command and a decision made. At Army Headquarters Max Hoffmann noted that: 'if things go well, Prittwitz will be seen as a great captain. If not, we will be the ones to shoulder the blame.' The question was how Prittwitz would react to the rapidly changing situation.

Ultimately, it would prove to be Generalleutnant Hermann von François, commanding I.Armee-Korps, whose actions would prove to be the trigger for what came next.

As his surname implies, François was descended from French Huguenots who had left their homeland following the revocation of the Edict of Nantes in 1685, his father and grandfather both serving as general officers in the Prussian army. In 1913, he had been asked by the General Staff to prepare a paper on the defence of East Prussia, suggesting that he consider the use of the latest technology as well as the state of the prospective enemy's command structure. He did so, advocating an aggressive forward deployment to hinder and disrupt the enemy's preparations. This potentially created the environment for him to make a fatal mistake, which would then be exploited and punished heavily. The proposals were warmly accepted, as was the suggestion that some of the province's garrison troops would be better used in forward positions rather than behind concrete or medieval brickwork. As a result, a battalion of infantry and a machine-gun company were transferred to bolster the garrison of Goldapp.

When he received the orders to pull back to the line of the Angerapp, François demurred and requested additional clarification, informing Prittwitz that the men under his command were proud East Prussians and that the proposed plan would simply abandon far too much territory to the enemy without a shot having been fired in its defence. The army commander was adamant that I.Armee-Korps was to withdraw from its position to join the rest of the army; whilst he admitted that – with the numbers of troops involved – there was a risk in his intended strategy, there was an even greater one in the course of action that François was suggesting – one which could, if things went especially badly, lead to the loss of a quarter of the army at a single stroke.

Believing that his orders were being followed, Prittwitz reiterated his instructions to the other units involved in the operation; even so, François made no move to comply with the orders that he had been given, his intent being to give battle where he stood. But François had his own problems: at corps level and above, a formation's chief of staff had the right to inform the next level of command when they felt that their own commander's conduct was detrimental to the service – and Colonel Schmidt von Schmidtseck, I.Armee-Korps' principal staff officer, was no admirer of his commander.

In order to prevent any information leaking back to the army headquarters, François hit on a novel solution: Schmidt was left in charge of corps headquarters at Insterburg, whilst he himself would personally 'confer' with his divisional commanders in the field, effectively becoming his own staff officer and removing any chance of Prittwitz finding out the truth of what was happening in I.Armee-Korps' sector.

STALLUPÖNEN: 17 AUGUST

Blatantly disobeying Prittwitz's orders, François deployed his troops around the railway junction at Stallupönen – I.Armee-Korps' 1.Infanterie-Division occupied the town itself, whilst 2.Infanterie-Division took up position to the south-west of the town, covering Goldapp and Tollmingkehmen, with Brecht's 1.Kavallerie-Division covering his rearward communications and Lupin's 2.Landwehr-Brigade covering the Memel River at Tilsit. François himself would remain with his headquarters and corps assets at Insterburg. As the troops moved into position, the first small skirmishes began to break out along the length of the frontier as parties from both sides made initial contact.

Having by now found out that one of his corps was significantly further to the east of where it should have been, and with the overwhelming possibility that these troops would soon encounter a significantly larger enemy force, Prittwitz ordered François to leave the detachments at Goldapp, Stallupönen and Tollmingkehmen and withdraw the bulk of his command to concentrate upon a defensive position at Gumbinnen, some 15 miles to the rear of his current position. But even had he been inclined to follow his superior's instructions, time for François, for now at least, was about to run out. Reports of enemy contact were increasing, with news arriving that the outlying German positions were already being pushed back towards Stallupönen. By the early morning of 17 August, Generalleutnant Richard von Conta – commander of 1.Infanterie-Division – had telephoned corps headquarters, advising of enemy attacks along his entire front.

Rushing 'to the sound of the guns', François ordered his artillery reserve to move up as fire support and then gave instructions for Generalleutnant Adalbert von Falk, his other divisional commander, to move troops up from Tollmingkehmen in order to threaten the open flank of the enemy column.

By midday, the German howitzers had deployed and were already in action, but there were only 16 of them. Whilst they were a welcome support, Conta estimated that his command was facing the leading divisions of at least three enemy corps, information that he imparted to François when the latter arrived in person shortly afterwards. In reality, the Germans at Stallupönen were facing the 25th and 27th divisions of Yepanchin's III Corps, with remaining elements of Rennenkampf's army conducting flanking moves on either side of the town. Simply put, the defenders' position was

The Battle of Stallupönen, 17 August 1914

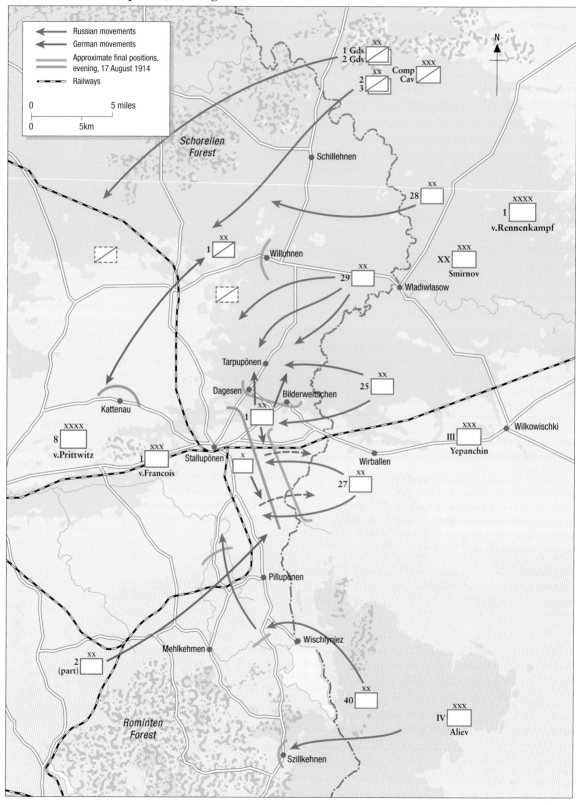

becoming increasingly precarious, and urgent action needed to be undertaken before it was too late – current tactical doctrine stating that if a formation was engaged too closely to withdraw in safety, it should launch local counter-attacks in order to trade space for time.

Destroyed artillery equipment abandoned on the battlefield, its nationality unknown. (Bundesarchiv, Bild 146-1976-006-20/CC-BY-SA 3.0, CC BY-SA 3.0 DE)

The immediate problem facing the two men was that, having already thrown everyone who could hold a rifle into the firing line, Conta was being constantly obliged to extend his lines outwards to ward off the Russian flanking moves and prevent his position from being encircled. As a result of this necessity, a dangerous gap had now developed in the centre of his position, one that was held by two thinly stretched companies of 41.Infanterie-Regiment, whilst elsewhere 43.Infanterie-Regiment were engaged on all sides, and if not relieved would soon be overrun. Aggressive action by both the 1st and 3rd Grenadiers achieved some limited initial success, but both regiments became bogged down in a series of isolated firefights, and it was at this time that the fates played an unexpected hand.

Initially unaware of I.Armee-Korps' exact position, Prittwitz had been attempting to reach François at Insterburg, only to be vaguely told that the general was with his staff, visiting the front lines. Incredulous, he immediately ordered that an officer be sent out to find the corps commander – wherever he might be – and order him, in the army commander's name, to immediately pull his forces back to Gumbinnen.

According to François' later account, whilst observing the battle from the church tower at Stallupönen, he was indeed confronted by an officer of his staff, who was forced to shout his message in order to made himself heard above the artillery fire: 'The Commanding General instructs General von François to break off the battle at once and retire upon Gumbinnen as previously instructed.' Given the confusion of battle, and François' own penchant for self-embellishment these may not actually have been Prittwitz's exact words, as, if he were unaware of François' location, he was logically unaware that the latter was in the middle of a battle. But this fits with the general's alleged reply when – according to his own, later, account – he told the hapless messenger to: 'Tell General von Prittwitz that General von François will break off the action once the enemy has been beaten and only then.'

Again, these may not be the exact words used, but even if they were, it was more than likely that they would have been diplomatically edited before being passed back up the chain of command, the message being relayed to army headquarters sometime around 1600hrs that afternoon.

To the south, and having heard the sound of heavy firing to the north, Falk had already made up his mind that his colleague was facing a superior enemy force, and had taken the decision to march to his assistance. Therefore, when he received François' instructions to move up in support of 1.Infanterie-Division, preparations for the move were already well underway.

A German Landsturm guardpost on the Polish-German border. These small outposts would provide crucial early warning of enemy activity. (Author's collection)

Leaving two infantry battalions of Boeß' 4.Infanterie-Brigade – supported by six guns – to hold their current position and maintain the links with the 3.Infanterie-Brigade in Goldapp, Falk moved off at around 1130hrs with his remaining six battalions supported by some 36 guns of Möves' 1.Feldartillerie-Brigade.

As his column approached Stallupönen, and unsure as to the exact situation facing him, Falk halted near the village of Todszuhnen to deploy his troops for combat before continuing his march cross-country to a point where he believed the German front line to be. Moving towards the sound of the fighting, he now found himself to be behind the flank of a large force of Russians – the 105th (or Orenburg) Regiment – pushing westwards in an attempt to turn the defenders' flank. As luck would have it, and at that time unbeknownst to either side, the German column had made its approach through an area that, if all had gone to plan, would have been occupied by overwhelming enemy forces.

It would appear that First Army's staff had undertaken no measures whatsoever in order to ensure that the three corps would advance in tandem, which meant that given a number of unexplained delays, the area which should have been occupied by the 40th Division of Aliev's IV Corps was in fact void of Russian troops. Thus, the further that Yepanchin's divisions actually advanced, the more exposed their left flank would increasingly become, a problem exacerbated by the fact that shortcomings in the Russian forces meant that almost all messages had to be transmitted by runner or dispatch rider. If this obvious negligence had not been grievous enough, the coming debacle was cemented by the fact that earlier that morning the official intelligence reports passed down from army headquarters had placed the whole of the German I.Armee-Korps at the railway junction, and thus Colonel Komarov, the commander of the 105th, was unwittingly leading his regiment against the flank of only a part of the enemy corps rather than that of the whole formation as anticipated.

Seizing the moment, Falk ordered his Füsilier-Regiment 33 and Infanterie-Regiment 45 to attack. Believing that this was simply the 'fog of war' and that the newcomers were from the 40th Division, Komarov halted his advance and sent some mounted officers to clarify the situation, but was

During a lull in the fighting, German soldiers are seen here receiving field post and reading newspaper reports. (Author's collection)

himself killed as the enemy poured fire into his stationary troops. Taking heart, the men of Conta's 2.Infanterie-Brigade launched their own attack, and, hit on both flanks, the Orenburg Regiment collapsed and broke in disorder – losing some 3,000 casualties, about three-quarters of its active strength. Continuing forward, Falk's infantry charged into the remainder of the 27th Division, causing severe casualties on both the 106th (Ufa) and 107th (Troitski) regiments, the disintegration stopping the Russian left flank dead in its tracks.

With the sudden and unexpected heavy losses – estimates would suggest almost 7,000 of all ranks, roughly 46 per cent of the divisional strength – and ammunition supplies running critically low, the battered riflemen disengaged and pulled back to reorganize and resupply. It would prove to be the last aggressive manoeuvre of the day.

Although it would understandably be overshadowed by the sheer scale of later events, and notwithstanding the measure of extreme luck which had enabled him to arrive on the battlefield exactly when and where he did, Falk's intervention at Stallupönen would prove to be one of the most critical actions of the Tannenberg campaign as a whole.

Pride before a fall: victorious Russian Infantry march through Insterburg. (Author's collection)

Conta's division was almost on its last legs, virtually surrounded and with casualties mounting as its ammunition supplies dwindled. The arrival of the corps artillery reserve – whilst it had admittedly kept German hopes alive – simply could not have turned the course of the battle on its own, and it was only Falk's arrival that had prevented François' pugnacity from developing into a major catastrophe. Although the empty corridor through which he had led his command had been due to enemy error, it is almost certain that had Falk not seized the initiative when he did and instead chosen to wait for orders, he would have arrived too late. As a result, the greater part of François' I.Armee-Korps and possibly even its commander would have been rendered *hors de combat*, not only leaving Prittwitz to face nine enemy corps with but three of his own, but also guaranteeing that his forces would – as a result – be spread so thin that the chances of a breakthrough by either of the Russian armies would be that much closer to becoming a certainty.

Oddly enough, the attitude on both sides after the battle was markedly different. For his part, and despite the heavy casualties his command had suffered so far, Yepanchin could sense victory and wanted to renew the combat as soon as was practicable, believing that he could clear the road ahead and open the way to Gumbinnen.

François, on the other hand, temporarily chastened by the combat and having seen at first hand the damage that had been meted out to his 1.Infanterie-Division, was more than aware that the enemy disengagement had been nothing more than a postponement of defeat. Accepting that to remain where he was would be to sacrifice his command to no real purpose, he decided to rejoin his headquarters at Insterburg. Before he did so, he gave orders for both of his division commanders to withdraw to the holding position at Gumbinnen. It was there, and indeed as per Prittwitz's previous instructions, that he now intended to make a stand and 'fight' his corps as a single unit rather than as separate detachments.

Upon his arrival, he naturally found a series of orders waiting for him. Having ridden his luck all day, the commander of I.Armee-Korps now telephoned Prittwitz, deciding to risk one last audacious throw of the dice. Before the latter could interrupt, François informed his commander that not only had he successfully beaten two enemy corps and thrown them back to the border, but that thanks to his successful management of the battle at Stallupönen, 8.Armee now had not only a far greater appreciation of the size, composition and intentions of the forces opposing it, but as

Russian cavalry troops ride through Tilsit. (Author's collection)

a result had also forged the weapon with which to secure victory.

Despite any antagonism that he might have felt to his mercurial subordinate, Prittwitz was more than aware that he was dealing with the only officer under his command who had the experience of commanding a major body of troops in a modern battle. François had, after all, commanded the only German forces to have taken part in a pitched battle since 1871.

Whilst the Germans withdrew under cover of darkness and the Russians moved stealthily forward through the fields to consolidate their hold on the outlying villages, a final scene was to be played out before the curtain fell on the Battle of Stallupönen. Earlier in the day, Conta had dispatched two companies of Infanterie-Regiment 41 to plug the gap in the centre of the German positions, but in the confusion of the retreat, no one had remembered to give them orders to abandon their exposed position and join in the withdrawal to Gumbinnen. They were still there several hours later, when the advancing enemy called on them to surrender. Having used up the last of their ammunition, the men fixed bayonets and awaited the inevitable attack, but surprisingly none came. A hurried conference between the company officers ensued, which concluded that a heroic death would serve no purpose, and instead whispered orders were given for the men to pull out. Marching as quickly as was practicable, the forlorn group rejoined their comrades the following day, earning cheers as they entered the German positions, accompanied by a number of bewildered Russian conscripts whom they had taken prisoner during their night march.

GUMBINNEN: 20 AUGUST

Both sides naturally viewed their experiences of 17 August differently. Despite having little or no knowledge of the size of the forces facing him, François had followed his instincts and sought to conduct the 'active' defence as prescribed by the Schlieffen Plan, but in doing so had almost led his corps to disaster. It was a salutary lesson and one that he vowed never to repeat. For Yepanchin, and despite both the operational failures that led the 27th Division into disaster and indeed the heavy losses inflicted on that formation, his green conscripts had not only met and defeated the enemy on its home soil, but more importantly he had secured the all-important rail hub that the First Army so urgently required if it were to improve its logistical capabilities as it advanced further into East Prussia.

At the higher level, both army commanders also had differing opinions as to the outcome of the initial battle for East Prussia. Removed from the front line, Prittwitz naturally feared that his opponent would take advantage of his overwhelming superiority in cavalry and launch an aggressive pursuit of the retreating I.Armee-Korps, but no such orders came. Having engaged in a series of small engagements with German outposts, the Russian cavalry simply unsaddled on the afternoon of 17 August and went into bivouac, thereby missing the second opportunity in a single day for the First Army to inflict a significant defeat on the enemy.

The Battle of Gumbinnen, 20 August 1914

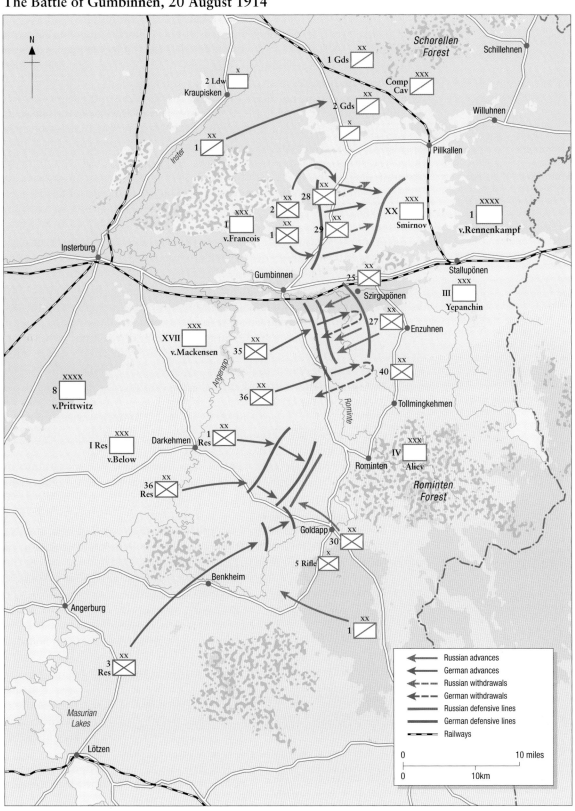

N

Schorellen Forest

Schillehnen

1 Gds xx

Comp Cav xxx

Willuhnen

2 Ldw x
Kraupisken

2 Gds xx

x

Pillkallen

1 xx

Inster

28 xx

2 xx

XX xxx
Smirnov

1 xxxx
v.Rennenkampf

I xxx
v.Francois

1 xx

29 xx

Insterburg

Gumbinnen

25 xx
Szirgupönen

Stallupönen

III xxx
Yepanchin

XVII xxx
v.Mackensen

35 xx

27 xx

Enzuhnen

Angerapp

36 xx

40 xx

Tollmingkehmen

8 xxxx
v.Prittwitz

Rominte

I Res xxx
v.Below

Darkehmen

1 Res xx

IV xxx
Rominten Aliev

Rominten Forest

36 Res xx

Goldapp

30 xx

5 Rifle x

Benkheim

Angerburg

1 xx

Masurian Lakes

3 Res xx

	Russian advances
	German advances
	Russian withdrawals
	German withdrawals
	Russian defensive lines
	German defensive lines
	Railways

Lötzen

0   10 miles

0   10km

For Rennenkampf, the inability to exploit his victory was a stain on his honour. The old adage was that a cavalryman should always have the point of his sword in a retreating enemy's back, but the unpalatable truth was that his men had been advancing steadily for the better part of a week in extremely arduous conditions. Not only did they need rest, but he also needed his supply columns to catch up with the main body, not just bringing food and ammunition but more importantly telephone and telegraph wire, which would improve communications up and down the chain of command. He therefore gave orders for the army to consolidate its position and advance towards the line of the Angerapp on 19 August, but that the following day, the 20th, would be a day of rest before embarking on the next stage of the campaign.

In order to offset François' obvious numerical disadvantage in the face of the enemy, Prittwitz authorized the release of the General Reserve from the Königsberg garrison to reinforce the troops at Gumbinnen. A division-sized formation of Landwehr and Ersatz (Replacement) units, together with the addition of several batteries of artillery, would enable I.Armee-Korps to mount a credible defence of the town.

Having fully comprehended his 'tactical blindness' both before and during the Battle of Stallupönen, and whilst he began his planning for the coming engagement, François now resolved to make full use of his greatest advantage over the enemy by sending the men and machines of Captain Heinrich's FFA 14 aloft on one reconnaissance mission after another. This persistence paid off when the airmen reported that although the enemy had halted some distance from Gumbinnen – doubtless to make their own preparations – it looked as if their right flank was 'open' and could be 'turned' by a determined manoeuvre. When this assumption was confirmed by a Zeppelin overflight, François knew that he had another opportunity for offensive action.

Eager to take the fight to the enemy, François called Prittwitz to inform him of the fresh opportunity that lay before him, advising that he intended to use Falk's 2.Infanterie-Division to envelop the enemy line in the early hours of 20 August and attack into its undefended flank. As his commanding officer digested this information, he added that there was an even greater opportunity for 8.Armee. Operational doctrine called for the massing of troops against a vulnerable enemy, and if Prittwitz would now consent to the redeployment of additional troops in support of his proposed attack, there would be the real opportunity for the Germans to defeat one of the two enemy thrusts, and drive Rennenkampf's army from the field. His idea was to employ a 'Cannae manoeuvre' with I.Armee-Korps turning the enemy's right flank and XVII./I.Reserve-Korps turning their left, whilst the General Reserve held Gumbinnen, fending off any Russian attacks while the regular formations encompassed the enemy's destruction.

Initially undecided, Prittwitz was eventually won over by François' confidence, authorizing the proposed manoeuvre and

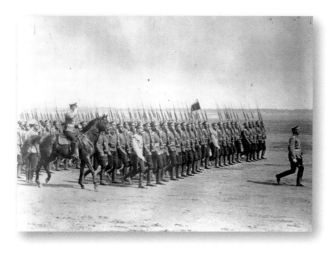
Russian infantry on parade. (Author's collection)

agreeing that Mackensen's XVII.Armee-Korps, together with Below's I.Reserve-Korps and 3.Reserve-Division would redeploy so that they would extend François' line southwards before Falk commenced his attack.

With the promised reinforcement, François' amended plan was simple but potentially devastating. Under cover of darkness, Falk's 2.Infanterie-Division would make a ten-mile night march in order to place it on the open Russian flank; and with the onset of daybreak they were to launch a surprise attack on the unsuspecting enemy encampments, and then – like beaters for a hunting party – drive them southwards onto the waiting guns of the German artillery. If Falk were successful, not only would he cause significant damage to the enemy, but he would also disrupt any enemy counter-attacks by continually pushing one opposing formation into the next as his command moved southwards.

Despite an initial scare caused by reports that the Russians had launched a surprise attack of their own, and disruption caused by a belt of heavy fog, Falk reached his assigned position on time, and deployed his brigades for the dawn attack.

As darkness turned to early morning dawn, the guns of Generalmajor Karl Fouquet's 2.Feldartillerie-Brigade began to thunder, sending shrapnel and explosive shells into the enemy bivouacs. The German infantry stormed forward into the rudely awoken men of Smirnov's XX Corps. The village of Mallwischken was quickly taken by Füsilier-Regiment 33, whilst elsewhere a detachment of Grenadier-Regiment 4 was able to engage a battery of artillery with close-range musketry, taking two guns and a number of men prisoner before it could safely disengage.

At first it looked as if the attack would be an unparalleled success, but the further they advanced, the more the attackers outdistanced their artillery support and the more that the Russian defences – based around small farms and villages – began to solidify. Raked by enemy fire the Germans advance slowed, but eventually regathered momentum, the troops pushing forward yard by yard until, sometime before midday, the grey wave lapped around the village of Uszballen, the focal point of Smirnov's defence. With regimental commanders needing to reorganize their men after several hours' intense combat before leading them forward, the settlement was taken street by street, building by building, with bullet, bayonet and rifle butt – many of the houses being set on fire in an attempt to force the defenders into abandoning their cover. It was an action that turned parts of the village into a charnel house, with those unwilling or unable to abandon their positions being consumed by the flames.

Further along the line, the next stage of François' battle plan fell into place when Conta's division began its own attack. At 0530hrs, and just as Falk's troops were making their presence felt, 1. and 2.Infanterie-Brigade began their advance against the Russian XX Corps' positions directly to their front, the movement being timed so as to pin their opponents in position, thereby adding to the confusion in the enemy ranks as Falk continued his drive southwards.

Eschewing the services of a tactical reserve, Conta committed his entire force to the attack, hoping to break through the enemy positions before they could rally. But unlike the flanking attack, the Russian forces in this sector, knowing that the Germans lay to their front, had earlier erected a series of rudimentary trenches and rifle pits for defence. These slowed the attackers, whose lines were galled by enemy fire, with mounted officers proving to be especially inviting targets for the defending riflemen. Progress was slow, the combat degenerating into a grinding affair, with the 28th Division of Smirnov's corps particularly unfortunate in being taken in the flank by Falk's attack from the north and then, as it turned to face its tormentors, being taken again in the flank, this time from the west. Fragmented and hit from several directions, the division disintegrated, leaving several thousand casualties – almost half its strength – on the field. Their doggedness under unrelenting pressure was later given respectful praise by their grey-clad opponents.

With one of Smirnov's divisions out of the fighting, it fell to the Russian 29th Division to restore the situation. This they did, mounting a series of vicious counter-attacks that were so successful in halting I.Armee-Korps' advance that Falk's artillery – having caught up with the rest of the command – began to bombard the area to their front at random, in the hope of breaking up the enemy attacks as they materialized, a task in which they more or less succeeded. Tragically, the area upon which they were firing was also occupied by their comrades in arms, and soon the men of 1.Infanterie-Division were fleeing towards their start lines in an effort to escape the friendly fire, whilst the Russian infantry used the confusion to disengage and retire to a secondary defence line. Although I.Armee-Korps would reform and occupy much of the enemy's start positions, the German artillery had effectively negated any chance of François' attack being as successful as he had originally predicted. Any success would now rest on the shoulders of the troops moving up against Rennenkampf's left flank.

The closest of the two – Mackensen's XVII.Armee-Korps less Infanterie-Regiment 129 – had set off on a 15-mile march at about 1800hrs the previous day, its progress being impeded by large numbers of refugees blocking the roads and bringing with them the inevitable rumours of enemy activity. As the columns marched through the night, there were inevitably large numbers of stragglers, and so, just before dawn, Mackensen gave the order to halt, intending to reform and rest his troops whilst he attempted to make contact with François to find out the latest situation.

During his approach march, Mackensen had been confidently assured that he would only encounter light opposition. As the sun rose, he ordered the FFA 17 to conduct a number of reconnaissance flights to confirm what lay ahead of him, but the reports that came back spoke only of encampments, carts and wagons, not of marching columns. Certain that he had indeed achieved the intended surprise, he now resolved to attack, a decision subsequently reinforced by the welcome news that his 'missing' regiment was on the way to re-join his command, its position having been assumed by elements of the I.Reserve-Korps, following in his wake.

Like Conta to the north, the size of the sector in which he was to operate obliged Mackensen to deploy his forces in a single line with a minimal reserve as they moved north-eastwards; they easily brushed aside the small number of enemy outposts that lay in their path. At 0900hrs a courier from François arrived at the 35.Infanterie-Division HQ, advising that his command had been in action since dawn and that, having launched a successful flank attack, Falk was now driving the disrupted enemy before him, pushing them

General August von Mackensen, commander of the German XVII.Armee-Korps, 8.Armee. (Author's collection)

southwards onto XVII.Armee-Korps' guns. All the general had to do in order to secure a significant victory was to realign his advance and drive north into the enemy rear.

Whether due to initiative or a lust for glory, Hennig – the divisional commander – immediately gave orders for his brigades to conform to François' suggestion, before passing the message onward to Mackensen's headquarters. Irrespective of Hennig's motivation, the decision would prove to be a grave error, both brigades being stopped dead by an eruption of enemy artillery fire, striking the German troops from three sides. Elsewhere, the men of Mackensen's other division – the 36th – came in for an even ruder surprise when they came upon a line of entrenchments manned in strength by the Russian 27th and 40th divisions.

General Otto von Below, commander of the German I.Reserve-Korps, 8.Armee. (Author's collection)

Taking increasing casualties, especially amongst officers and NCOs 'leading from the front', the grey-clad infantry rushed forward in sections, intent on closing the range in order to gain the fire superiority dictated by their training, which would then lead to a bayonet charge to take the enemy position. Once in position, and after an exchange of musketry, the Germans stood up and charged, their losses increasing with each yard gained, and soon they were in amongst the enemy trenches, with numbers of the defenders being shot or bayoneted as they attempted to surrender to men who had just seen many of their friends and comrades fall.

Despite their success in overrunning the enemy position, the attackers' cohesion simply broke down. Some of them immediately began to dig in, using the enemy works for their own defence, whilst others simply stood there, uncertain of what to do, the links of their chain of command lying in the bloody fields behind them.

Movement of any description drew immediate enemy fire, and by midday Mackensen was sobered by the knowledge that his glorious advance had been halted by a well-prepared enemy and that his troops were pinned down along their entire front, unable to advance or withdraw without taking heavy losses. Having committed almost his entire command to the attack, he had but one reserve available to him – Infanterie-Regiment 129, which had only just arrived on the battlefield. Its commander, Oberst Ludwig Breßler, was now ordered to find and turn the enemy's left flank, thereby relieving pressure on the remainder of the corps whilst Mackensen considered his options. His

German infantry moving up to the front line. Both sides suffered terribly in the hot summer conditions, with many men suffering from heat exhaustion or sunstroke. (Author's collection)

choices were decreasing rapidly. Machine-gun companies had been rushed to the front line to add their fire to that of the rifle companies, but many were quickly silenced by Russian sharpshooters. The artillery proved to be just as ineffective, with the field guns unable to engage the enemy trenches, and there were simply too few howitzers to either provide covering fire whilst the troops moved or to act in a counterbattery role. The gunners' frustration at being unable to fulfil their task was given voice by Generalmajor Hahndorff of 36.Feldartillerie-Brigade when he asked bitterly: 'If the infantry insist

Illustration from *The London Sphere* showing Russian infantry storming a German gun battery at Gumbinnen. (Author's collection)

on continuing to advance like madmen, then how can they expect the Artillery to follow?'

Mackensen's hopes were soon dashed, as Breßler's attack foundered against a series of Russian strongpoints. The XVII.Armee-Korps' battle reached its nadir when the heavy howitzers of Fußartillerie-Regiment 11 deployed for action in support of 36.Infanterie-Division; after an initial salvo which landed in the 'no man's land' between the opposing troops, it tragically dropped the second and third salvoes directly upon the friendly troops with devastating effect. As if in atonement, two batteries of field artillery then rushed up to the front line in order to provide direct fire support, but like the machine gunners earlier, they were simply shot to pieces by Russian small-arms fire.

With his options dwindling, any remaining thoughts that Mackensen may have had of salvaging his command from the looming debacle and continuing the attack were rendered moot when his two divisions abandoned their forward positions and disengaged, their progress unmolested by enemy fire.

Earlier that morning XVII.Armee-Korps had mustered roughly 30,000 effectives, and by evening almost a third of that number had become either casualties, prisoners or were reported missing. Until it could rest, refit and reorganize, its future part in the campaign would be negligible. Whilst the northern pincer of François' planned attack had enjoyed a reasonable amount of success, the southern pincer had ended in defeat and near disaster. Although the Battle of Gumbinnen was effectively at an end, the final curtain had yet to fall on the day's fighting.

Having been given orders to advance to the town of Goldapp and from there to cover XVII.Armee-Korps' right flank, the men of von Below's I.Reserve-Korps had spent much of the previous evening moving along secondary roads, contesting their passage with the same groups of refugees that had earlier caused problems for Mackensen. This caused similar results, and forced Below to order a halt at about 0330hrs on the morning of the 20th in order to rest his command and rally any straggling elements. Three hours later, the men shouldered their packs once more and the columns began trudging northwards again. Unlike the line formations, I.Reserve-Korps had no aerial assets, and the opportunity was taken to send one of the two cavalry regiments to scout the road ahead.

Having approached to within a few miles of Goldapp, the German cavalrymen reported that they had seen no trace of any enemy troops – a state of affairs that led Below to conclude that, with the sounds of fighting audible in the distance, he would serve the army best not by merely covering Mackensen's right flank but rather by bringing his troops into action alongside their comrades of XVII.Armee-Korps. Communicating his intentions to 8.Armee HQ, and issuing the requisite orders to his two divisions, Below was given the unwelcome news that earlier that morning, elements of FFA 16 had confirmed the movement of significant numbers of Russian troops heading north around Goldapp. Undeterred, and believing that he would still be coming into position behind the enemy, he gave orders for the march to continue, seemingly omitting to instruct his cavalry screen to continue with aggressive patrolling – a lack of application which would soon have dire consequences.

As the troops halted for a rest stop near the village of Klezowen, the men of 1.Reserve-Division observed a cloud of dust off to their right. With the troops obscured by the shimmering heat, a detachment of Garde-Reserve-Ulanen-Regiment 1 was sent out to ascertain their identity. The answer was not long in coming, when a number of saddles were emptied by rifle fire, and the remaining cavalrymen rode back pell-mell for the safety of their own lines.

The warning came too late, as lines of khaki-clad troops rose up, seemingly from nowhere – testament to the Russian abilities in the use of cover and concealment – and began firing into the dispersed knots of field-grey infantry, the staccato rifle reports being punctuated by the heavier boom of Russian field guns. Their previous lacklustre performance at Stallupönen notwithstanding, the men of Aliev's IV Corps had managed to successfully ambush the German column, pinning it in position and preventing it from taking part in the action to the north at Gumbinnen.

Supported by Aliev's heavy artillery reserve, Kolyanovsky's 30th Infantry Division thrust forward in a series of coordinated attacks that pushed the Germans back on their heels, gradually silencing any batteries that had been moved forward to provide close fire support. At his field headquarters, Below debated his choices: if a single enemy division were attacking his command, it was certain that a second was in close proximity. If he were to commit the remainder of his command to the developing action, he could easily find himself disadvantaged by a second Russian attack, yet if he opted to husband his remaining resources in anticipation of such an eventuality, he would undoubtedly be sacrificing one of his two divisions for an uncertain outcome.

For an officer with little practical experience, but lengthy service, Below's decision was automatic – 36.Reserve-Division was committed to the hitherto uneven battle, and gradually the Russian attack began to ebb and the situation stabilized. Re-forming, the Germans now went over to the attack, but a combination of losses and the fact that reserve formations deployed only half of the number of guns as their comrades in the line – meant that many of these were conducted without artillery support, degenerating into a series of disconnected infantry engagements. With the Russian gunners unwilling to cause unnecessary friendly casualties by targeting enemy units in close proximity to their own troops, the German advantage in numbers now began to tell, and, as darkness fell, Kolyanovsky ordered his men to disengage.

If victory is measured by possession of the battlefield, then despite the enemy's initial success, Below had indeed won his battle. But balanced against that was the mauling that his command had taken at enemy hands, especially the losses inflicted on his already limited complement of artillery. In addition to this, his command was badly dispersed and needed to reorganize before the enemy could resume its attack the following morning. Defeat had been staved off, but not fully averted.

François' original proposal to Prittwitz had called for 8.Armee to conduct a battle of envelopment comprising three interlinked components, but what it had actually done was to fight three distinctly separate engagements, only one of which – that in the I.Armee-Korps sector – could be regarded as an unqualified success, and even there the German losses had been high.

GUMBINNEN, 20 AUGUST 1914 (PP. 42–43)

For both sides, the initial clashes of the campaign in East Prussia would prove to be a sharp lesson in the realities of modern warfare as opposed to the theories of the training manual. The Germans in particular were discomfited by the Russian troops' use of terrain in both offensive and defensive situations, a skill which would later manifest itself in German reports that the Russians had been siting carriage-mounted machine guns in the upper branches of trees.

Another departure from the training manual was that, on several occasions, German artillery commanders were obliged to bring their guns dangerously close to the front line in order to effectively engage the enemy and offer close fire support, which led one officer to wryly comment that it was the infantry that was supporting the artillery and not vice versa.

Based upon contemporary accounts of the Battle of Gumbinnen, here we see a detachment of Colonel Alexander Yarminsky's 3rd (Elisavetgrad) Hussars (3rd Cavalry Division, III Corps, **1**) overrunning a battery of German 77mm field guns (**2**). The mainstay of the German *Feldartillerie*, the 7.7cm FK96 n.A. was an updated version of the original 1896 version that had been introduced in 1905 in order to 'phase out' the earlier model, and would itself be replaced by a more modern weapon that would be developed during the course of the war.

Although such attacks were effectively of a 'hit and run' nature – the horsemen naturally being unable to maintain their position so close to the enemy lines without close infantry support – the fact that they were made at all severely curtailed the effectiveness of the German artillery. Mackensen's XVII.Armee-Korps was to lose a number of guns in such a manner before the situation could be salvaged and the line stabilized.

A CHANGE OF STRATEGY

For possibly the last time during his brief tenure of command, fate smiled favourably upon Prittwitz when XX.Armee-Korps reported that FFA 15 had been flying continuous reconnaissance sorties above Second Army, observing that Samsonov's forces had remained more or less in position during the day, without signs of any tell-tale build up of troops preparatory to an advance. This naturally meant that he was now free to concentrate on the situation in the north, and as a result he requested full situation reports from his three corps commanders in order that he could make a reasoned decision. In the interim, contrary reports came in, this time from the fortress of Graudenz, suggesting that instead of maintaining his position, Samsonov was actually advancing.

Opinion at army headquarters was by now deeply divided. Prittwitz was considering a withdrawal behind the line of the Vistula, but a number of his more aggressively minded subordinates suggested that the Russians in the south would soon outrun their logistical chain and be forced to halt, which would give 8.Armee the necessary time to comprehensively defeat Rennenkampf before it redeployed to deal with Samsonov.

In theory, it was a viable proposition, but it was not only a course of action that was predicated on the Second Army being forced to halt, but was also one that failed to take into account the physical and attritional losses that the three German corps had suffered over the previous days. Despite both Mackensen and Below playing down their actual losses, it was abundantly clear that neither formation would be able to take the field for at least 24 hours, a period which would give Rennenkampf a sufficient 'window of opportunity' within which to launch his own attack.

We are told that a number of robust arguments now moved back and forth – many of these only coming to light in memoirs written long after the battle had been won – and several considerations would influence Prittwitz's final decision.

Firstly, as the enemy had not been as comprehensively defeated as François' original plan had suggested he would be, there was naturally no guarantee that a second day of fighting would achieve the original objective. Secondly, Prittwitz had to consider the extent of the losses taken in the recent fighting. Thirdly, unless any continued engagement yielded anything other than a comprehensive victory, the continued presence of the General Reserve in the field represented a threat to the security of Königsberg. Fourthly and finally, Rennenkampf had at his disposal an overwhelming superiority in cavalry, which effectively meant that – all discussion as to the effectiveness of modern weapons in defence aside – he had the capacity to overrun the German lines of communication and supply, an implicit threat which compromised 8.Armee's capacity to operate in the field.

As a result – and in his eyes acting in accordance with the established strategic plan – Prittwitz ordered that the General

Masters of concealment: Russian infantry engaging the enemy from a prone firing position. (Author's collection)

Reserve return to Königsberg whilst the three corps redeployed to the south-west in order that the army could mass against Samsonov's forces.

Movement orders were to be drafted for I.Armee-Korps to pull back and entrain for a rail movement that would bring it into the line via Deutsch-Eylau. The 3.Reserve-Division would make a similar movement towards Allenstein, the two formations taking station upon XX.Armee-Korps' right and left flanks respectively. With Scholtz's line thus strengthened, Mackensen and Below would follow in the wake of 3.Reserve-Division and take up a mutually supporting position from where they could engage either of the two Russian armies, as circumstances dictated. Finally, Brecht's 1.Kavallerie-Division was given the task of masking Rennenkampf's army, giving the illusion that the German forces in the area were significantly greater than a thin cavalry screen.

Having made his decision, Prittwitz now had to fight his own personal battle, one which would prove to be as arduous as the one fought by the troops in the front line. Throughout the late morning and early afternoon, the OHL in Koblenz had been receiving continuous and upbeat reports from East Prussia, depicting 8.Armee as being on the cusp of a spectacular victory. But now, when he telephoned the chief of staff, the army commander had to inform Moltke that the situation was dire, and that having 'shot its bolt', his forces would be in the gravest danger if they remained in position. Stressing that they were in accordance with the established plan of operations, he outlined his plans and ended the call believing that the matter had been settled.

Overnight, things were to change dramatically for the worse. An evening communique to OHL would prove to be the first spark, when it transpired that in summarizing the movement orders, the message had incorrectly stated that the army was redeploying to West Prussia, in other words beyond the Vistula, and implying a tacit abandonment of East Prussia. Things got worse when Prittwitz, after an uneasy night's sleep, suggested that XVII. and I.Reserve-Korps would no longer move as previously decided but should remain on the Angerapp to counter any enemy attempt to exploit the German withdrawal. When advised of this, Moltke was apoplectic, coming to the conclusion that not only was Prittwitz planning a general retreat, but that in doing so was intent on dividing his forces in the face of the enemy at exactly the time when he should have been concentrating them – not only ignoring a military truism, but also the established plan, which called for the massing of force to exploit a detached enemy's weakness and defeat him. To the Army's chief of staff, it mattered not if the intended target was the Niemen or the Narew army; what mattered was a complete adherence to the plan and its justification in the form of a decisive victory.

Throughout 21 August, officers had been communicating with OHL, when François, once again, overstepped his position and, following peacetime practice, communicated his own version of events directly to the Kaiser – who naturally lost no time in raising the matter with Moltke. But the final nail in Prittwitz's coffin came in the form of a telephone call between his chief of staff Georg von Waldersee and Hermann von Stein, the quartermaster-general at OHL. During their conversation, Stein 'suggested' that 8.Armee should continue to operate against Rennenkampf's army, citing the fact that it would be unable to resupply as quickly as the German forces and thus be at a severe disadvantage in any prolonged fighting. Waldersee prevaricated, reiterating Prittwitz's intentions; the further Stein pressed him, the more entrenched in his repetition he became.

Screening Russian First Army and manoeuvre against Second Army

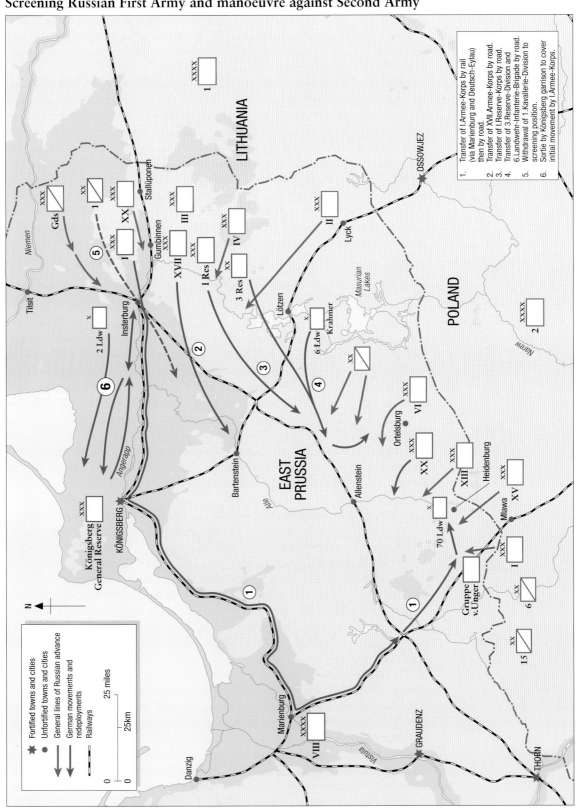

Legend:
- ★ Fortified towns and cities
- ● Unfortified towns and cities
- General lines of Russian advance
- German movements and redeployments
- Railways

0 — 25km
0 — 25 miles

N

Box text:
1. Transfer of I.Armee-Korps by rail (via Marienburg and Deutsch-Eylau) then by road.
2. Transfer of XVII Armee-Korps by road.
3. Transfer of I.Reserve-Korps by road.
4. Transfer of 3.Reserve-Division and 6.Landwehr-Infanterie-Brigade by road.
5. Withdrawal of 1.Kavallerie-Division to screening position.
6. Sortie by Königsberg garrison to cover initial movement by I.Armee-Korps.

In the German Army, one of the tasks of a chief of staff is to offer counsel and advice in order to prevent their commanding officer from making rash or precipitate decisions, but as Moltke and Stein convened to discuss their respective conversations with 8.Armee's most senior officers, it was clear to both men that drastic measures would need to be taken to salvage a situation that was, in their opinion, close to spiralling out of control. With the stagnating situation on the Western Front demanding increasing amounts of their time and attention, events in East Prussia – whilst important in their own right – were a diversion that OHL could simply not afford. Both Prittwitz and Waldersee would need to go, being replaced by men who could be trusted to act on their own initiative with the forces available to them and use these resources to achieve the results required.

The problem was that this would need to be achieved before events were overtaken by developments on the Eastern Front. Luckily enough, one man was already waiting in the wings: Generalmajor Erich Ludendorff, who was already being known as *Der Held von Lüttich*, the Hero of Liège.

MAN OF THE MOMENT

On the evening of 21 August, Ludendorff received notification of his transfer to the staff of 8.Armee, and was told to present himself at OHL the following morning for a conference with Moltke before travelling east to assume his new role. The invitation read: 'Of course, you will not be held responsible for that which has already happened, but with your energy, I am confident that you can prevent the worst from happening in the future … So, answer this new call, it is the greatest compliment that can be paid to any soldier in time of war.'

Stein also wrote to Ludendorff, concluding his note with the words: 'You must accept, and go to East Prussia. The interests of the state make this imperative. Your task will be a difficult one, but I am certain that you will prove equal to it.'

His actions at Liège notwithstanding, Ludendorff was perhaps uniquely placed for the position in which he was to find himself. Having served as a staff officer under Schlieffen, he had taken part in various staff rides and wargames in East Prussia and was thus more than familiar with both the tactical and strategic precepts which the High Command required for the conduct of the war in the east. As soon as he arrived at Koblenz, he was ushered into Moltke's presence to be briefed on the situation facing 8.Armee – Prittwitz's intended 'abandonment' of East Prussia leaving the various isolated fortresses and garrisons to represent Germany's sole forward defence in the face of the Russian advance.

Taking his time to study the various maps and leaf through the latest reports received at OHL, Ludendorff looked up at the two senior officers and bluntly stated that the decision to disengage and consolidate had been the correct one. Before either Moltke or Stein could react, however, he raised his hand to forestall any outburst on their part.

Continuing, he stressed that whilst this was the correct tactical decision based upon the locally contending forces, it was the incorrect strategic decision for the following reasons. Firstly, there was no guarantee that the suggested Line of the Vistula could be held against such odds. Secondly, it would have weakened 8.Armee's ability to support and act in concert with the Austrian armies operating to the south. It also bore no correlation to the current political situation, as it would require the abandonment of large areas of German territory, something that was unacceptable both to Berlin and to himself personally, especially in light of as yet unsubstantiated reports of Russian atrocities against the civilian population. In conclusion, Ludendorff stated that whilst the situation looked undeniably bleak, it was in no way unsalvageable.

Asked what he would do, 8.Armee's new chief of staff stated that any thought or comment of withdrawal should be publicly quashed whilst the redeployments suggested by Prittwitz should continue to be implemented. The reason for this was that, in his opinion, the most latent enemy threat was obviously the Narew Army, which was currently in a position to drive a wedge through German territory and cut 8.Armee off from both Pomerania and West Prussia. In the north the city of Königsberg was well garrisoned, and a siege could only be to the Germans' advantage as it would divert a significant part of Rennenkampf's army from offensive operations for little tangible gain. More than that, he would not be drawn upon, saying that he needed to be at army headquarters, reviewing and evaluating the situation at first hand.

Moltke concurred and, ordering Stein to give the necessary instructions in his name, informed Ludendorff as to the identity of his new commander. Given the need for an experienced officer, and the fact that it would be impractical to transfer one from front-line service, he had made his choice from the list of retired generals, deciding upon General der Infanterie Paul von Beneckendorff und von Hindenburg, an officer who had previously been a candidate for the position he himself now held.

At the time of the present meeting, Hindenburg had still to signal his acceptance of the position, but it was hoped that he would do so shortly and at Hanover would board the special train that was being put at Ludendorff's disposal for the journey to East Prussia.

The meeting at an end, Moltke informed Ludendorff that he had one more duty to perform before a car would take him to the railway station. Ushered into an adjoining room, he found himself in the presence of His Imperial Majesty Kaiser Wilhelm II who, after presenting Ludendorff with the Pour le Mérite, indulged him with some small talk before sweeping out with his entourage whilst the general went down to the waiting car, and thence to the railway station. There, and as the train was making ready to leave, he was informed that Hindenburg had accepted the appointment, and that he would be joining him during the early hours of the following morning. A full briefing of the situation in the east would be appreciated at Ludendorff's earliest possible convenience.

At 0400hrs on 22 August, the train pulled into Hanover and Hindenburg stepped aboard, meeting directly with Ludendorff, who was busily assimilating the latest situation reports. As the new army commander pored over the map,

Both sides profited from captured *matériel* and equipment. Here we see German Landwehr mounted on captured Russian horses. (Author's collection)

Hindenburg, Ludendorff, their staff and liaison officers. (Bundesarchiv, Bild 146-1993-132-12A/CC-BY-SA 3.0, CC BY-SA 3.0 DE)

he was advised that any plans for a withdrawal beyond the Vistula had been abandoned and that a new tactical position, oriented along the Passarge River, had been established in conjunction with the suggestions that Ludendorff had made at OHL. With that, both men retired to bed.

At each successive railway station along their route, further updates from army headquarters were received and reviewed. By 1400hrs on 23 August, when their train finally steamed into Marienburg, both generals had as accurate an overview of 8.Armee's position as could be obtained without their physical presence in the theatre of operations. All major formations were in their designated positions, and the whole situation rested on events in the northern sector, and on the level of Rennenkampf's activity, or indeed his inactivity.

Whilst Ludendorff had no fears for the security of the city itself, if the Russian First Army were to continue advancing west towards Königsberg, such a move would ultimately place him on 8.Armee's open left flank and create the possibility of an enemy drive south-west, parallel to the coast. The latter would take him into the German rear, threatening the West Prussian hinterland and, ultimately, Berlin. Alternately, should the Russian commander opt to continue directly south in pursuit of XX.Armee-Korps and I.Reserve-Korps, the combination of both Russian armies would serve not only to force the German forces to abandon all territory east of the Vistula – the very same offence for which Prittwitz had been sacked – but would also remove any possibility of 8.Armee being able to mass against either of the enemy forces as dictated by the German war plan.

Simply put, the course of the next – and arguably the most crucial – phase of the campaign no longer rested directly in German hands. The initiative lay firmly with the Russian commanders and how they would react in the wake of the Battle of Gumbinnen.

SAMSONOV'S PROGRESS

Having had the greatest distance to cover before reaching his initial start lines, with part of his command still forming up, and coupled with a series of hurried last-minute changes of plan, it was inevitable the men of Samsonov's Second Army would begin offensive operations after their compatriots in the Niemen Army had not only moved into enemy territory, but had also crossed swords with the foe. An additional reason for this delay was naturally the nature of Samsonov's orders. Whilst Rennenkampf's corps were concentrated on a relatively narrow front, the Second Army was obliged to operate over a much larger area. This naturally meant that communications between the army HQ and its subordinate corps, and indeed between the corps themselves, was often difficult. The shortage of telegraph or telephone wire meant that much-needed wheeled transport was used for the transmission of orders instead of for more pressing purposes such as reconnaissance, a task which devolved by necessity either on the limited number of aircraft available, the half-hearted participation of cavalry regiments or – as was more likely – infantrymen using impressed horseflesh or civilian transport to increase their mobility. If this were not enough, the Russian staff officers had to contend with the fact that instead of a single common volume, there were in fact several codebooks in service, and that there was no guarantee that either the sender or the recipient had access to the same code. This meant that, in acceptance of the fact that they could undoubtedly be intercepted by the enemy, a number of messages were transmitted in 'clear', the only way in which receipt could be relatively guaranteed.

Samsonov's immediate intention was to push forward and occupy a line from Mlawa to Ortelsberg via Neidenburg and Willenburg, with the 15th and 4th Cavalry divisions covering the army's flanks and the 6th Cavalry Division held as a general reserve. This would mean that having successfully bypassed the southern extremities of the Masurian Lakes, he would anchor his right flank on the Johannisburg Forest and present a solid, unfractured line to the enemy, which he knew was deployed somewhere to his front. If Rennenkampf were to be successful in the north, there remained sufficient scope for his rightmost corps to cooperate with First Army, but if something untoward had happened to the Niemen Army, he would still be in a strong enough position to drive through any enemy forces that confronted him.

By 21 August, as the armies in the north were reorganizing themselves after their exertions at Gumbinnen, Second Army's ad hoc reconnaissance efforts had confirmed the likely presence of enemy forces in at least two of the objective towns – Neidenburg and Ortelsburg – although it was more than likely that all four were occupied. This information was passed immediately by Samsonov up the chain of command to Zhilinski, who wanted him to make an immediate series of attacks along the line in order to take the enemy positions by storm. But the front commander was hundreds of miles away, and, to him, the Second Army was merely a number of coloured pins on a map. Samsonov, on the other hand, was the 'man on the ground' and he could see both the terrain before him, and the condition of his troops who had been forced-marching to reach their current positions, stretching their logistical chain to almost breaking point. For him, there was no question of his launching a frontal assault upon a line of towns and villages whose defensive states were a distinctly unknown quantity. Instead, he proposed that demonstrations be made against Neidenburg and Ortelsburg with a view to bypassing both positions and rendering their defence untenable. The premise was that if this were to succeed, the enemy would also be obliged to abandon the remaining towns, and Samsonov would be able to secure his objectives at minimal cost.

The fact of the matter is that none of the positions were actually occupied, and that when reports of the enemy advance reached XX.Armee-Korps' outposts, its regimental commanders began to send out their own reconnaissance parties. In one incident, a cycle detachment of the Infanterie-Regiment 151 engaged a Russian patrol on the outskirts of Neidenburg, where – after a sharp firefight – they took possession of a map showing the line of the intended Russian advance from the body of a dead Cossack officer. Their opponents withdrew post-haste with the news that the countryside was up in arms and that they had been ambushed by armed civilians.

During a lull in the fighting, a senior officer decorates German soldiers for bravery in the field. (Author's collection)

The Russian response was devastating, with Lieutenant-General Martos, commander of XV Corps, ordering his artillery to shell the town in an effort to disperse these *francs-tireurs* and ensure a rapid surrender of the town by the local authorities. By the time that the bombardment had finished, some 300 shells had been fired into the town and almost half of its buildings heavily damaged or destroyed. Satisfied that the inhabitants had taken the salutary lesson to heart, Martos then ordered the occupation of Neidenburg, which would be held by Russian forces until Second Army's collapse just over a week later.

For Samsonov, a combination of the initial reports received regarding the action at Gumbinnen together with the capture of Neidenburg and Ortelsburg seemed to indicate that the enemy collapse had been both greater and faster than anyone had at first thought, and thus warranted an immediate re-evaluation of the Russian plan. There was no further military necessity in redeploying troops in order to pin the enemy against the Masurian Lakes if he were no longer there. He therefore felt confident in once again amending his plans, this time shifting his line of advance even further to the west, a move which further reduced any chance of mutual cooperation between the two Russian armies. His prepared argument was that such cooperation had been clearly defined during the pre-planning stages of the campaign as being more of a strategic nature rather than a tactical one. If, therefore, as a result of his change of plans, he drew enemy troops upon himself that at present were facing the Niemen Army, then this was the best and most practical service that he could offer Rennenkampf.

With this in mind, Samsonov drafted orders for 23 August by which VI Corps would remain in position around Ortelsburg, acting as flank security, whilst – in the centre – XIII Corps would push onward to Jedwabno with XV Corps moving forward to a position between Frankenau and Orlau. The army's left flank would be refused slightly, with I Corps moving up as far as Soldau, and the three cavalry divisions maintaining their current positions relative to the advance.

Just as Moltke had been during his final conversations with Prittwitz, Zhilinski – in St Petersburg – was incandescent when he was apprised of the intended departure from the agreed plan. Samsonov's assertions that the move would not only threaten communications between both Prussia and the rest of Germany, but would also improve his own supply situation with the seizure of the railhead at Soldau, fell on deaf ears. His mood changed appreciably, however, when reports of the glorious victory at Gumbinnen were received from First Army's newly established field headquarters. With visions of catching the bulk of the enemy forces, rather than just a part, in a massive pincer movement, Zhilinski ordered that with the exception of I Corps – which would remain on station around Soldau to cover its left flank – the remainder of Second Army would now move directly north. In deference to the army commander's complaints about the physical condition of his men, they were to be in position on a line stretching eastwards from

Allenstein to Sensburg, by 26 August at the latest. As the man on the spot, Samsonov knew that his fulfilment of Zhilinski's instructions could only be conditional, as to comply with them he would need to march his troops through the Allensteiner Stadtforst, a large area of forest and lakes to the south of the eponymous town. All he could do was to continue with his own planned advance with the intent of bypassing the lakes before moving north and approaching Allenstein from the south-west.

On the evening of 22 August, his orders – already drafted before his telephone conversation with Zhilinski – were issued, with XIII and XV Corps and 2nd Infantry Division (of XXIII Corps) to be on the march before daybreak.

DER ALTE HASE

When Prittwitz ordered the XVII.Armee-Korps and I.Reserve-Korps to move north and join I.Armee-Korps around Gumbinnen, the task of facing off against the Russian Second Army fell upon the shoulders of General der Artillerie Friedrich von Scholtz, the commander of XX.Armee-Korps.

An officer with over 40 years' service behind him – in German military parlance *Ein Alte Hase* (literally, 'an old hare') – Scholtz was a gunner by trade, less thrusting than François and less dashing than Mackensen, but nonetheless an officer who took his craft seriously. He believed that the defence of East Prussia would be best achieved by science rather than élan, the key being to block the enemy's ability to manoeuvre, and then destroy him with firepower.

Whilst their commander had been born in Flensburg in Schleswig-Holstein, the men of XX.Armee-Korps – which had only been called to the colours in October 1912 – were all locals, almost all of them coming from the towns and villages over which they would soon be called to fight. They thus had a local knowledge second to none, something which would stand them in good stead in the coming days.

Aerial and terrestrial reconnaissance would confirm what Scholtz already knew. Even with the inclusion of additional troops drawn from either the Vistula fortresses or the various local Landwehr, Landsturm or Ersatz units, he simply didn't have enough men to mass against even a section of the approaching enemy, assuming, that is, that the remainder would be so poorly handled as to allow him to make such an attempt. As the enemy advanced, therefore, he withdrew his forces northwards into a compact defensive position based on an east–west line from Gilgenburg to Lahna, confident in his ability to fulfil his orders, stating: 'This command does not count on receiving any reinforcement as this command does not require any reinforcement. The main thing is the victory in the north. We will hold the enemy on this line.'

His confidence notwithstanding, Scholz was still in a fairly precarious position. Greatly outnumbered by the approaching Russian army, the only elements under his command which could be relied upon in open battle were the two divisions of his own XX.Armee-Korps. The remainder of his troops,

General Friedrich von Scholtz, commander of XX.Armee-Korps, 8.Armee. (Author's collection)

no matter how eager for combat, were best suited for the defence, manning and holding defensive positions, bloodying the enemy and then, if necessary, withdrawing to a secondary position in order to hopefully repeat the process. His other problem was, naturally enough, that under no circumstances could he trade space for time. His room to manoeuvre was finite, for if he withdrew more than once, it would not only open Danzig and Pomerania to the enemy, but would almost certainly compromise the continued existence of 8.Armee. In short, for XX.Armee-Korps and its supporting units, failure to hold the line was not an option.

Scholtz's new defensive position took the best possible advantage of the local terrain, one which mitigated much of the numerical disparity between his command and the approaching enemy. On his extreme right flank, a division of fortress troops under Generalmajor Fritz von Unger was dug in behind the Welle River, its flanks anchored upon two lakes, the Rumian See and the Große Damerau See. Next in line, 41.Infanterie-Division occupied a position extending from Unger's location eastwards towards the Kownatken See, on either side of which was deployed a regiment from Breithaupt's mixed 70.Landwehr-Brigade. The line continued eastwards with 37.Infanterie-Division holding an eight-mile line from Michalken through Frankenau towards Lykusen, anchoring the German left flank on the marshy headwaters of the Alle River, with forward positions established in the villages of Orlau and Lahna.

To the north of the main position, he would soon have the services of the infantry of Generalleutnant Kurt von Morgen's 3.Reserve-Division, which was at that moment in the process of detraining at Allenstein, having been transferred from the Gumbinnen area.

LAHNA AND ORLAU: 23–24 AUGUST

With the heavily forested terrain between them precluding any form of conventional reconnaissance, and whilst Samsonov was obliged to drive his men on, trudging blindly forward along winding wooded paths in a direction that they believed would take them into contact with the enemy, Scholtz – with a superior aerial capability – was the recipient of continually updated reports as to Russian movements. These came from observation flights, and also from when the airship Zeppelin Z-V, having lost altitude whilst on patrol south of Orlau, was subjected to a mass of Russian small-arms fire.

Despite this advantage, and having established his headquarters at Mühlen, a village roughly equidistant from both ends of his line, all Scholtz could do now was to wait until the enemy made his move and then react. Committed to a static defence, his only option was to 'ride out' any enemy attacks and then counter them with his limited tactical reserves. Moreover, he had by now been advised that because of an 'opportunity' for the corps of Mackensen and Below to combine against a seemingly isolated Russian VI Corps, they would no longer be taking up position on his left flank. No sooner had it completed its training than Scholtz ordered 3.Reserve-Division to close up on XX.Armee-Korps by moving south-west towards Grieslienen.

By late morning, elements of the Russian 6th and 8th divisions were pushing through the villages of Salusken and Radomin, their leading elements constructing a series of rifle pits under full view of the German lines. Under the cover of sporadic rifle fire from these positions, further khaki-clad troops made their way forward. At 1400hrs, as the German positions were rocked by the continuous impact of artillery shells, the Second Army made its move with both divisions, now joined by XXIII Corps' 2nd Infantry Division, advancing upon von Staabs' thinly stretched 37.Infanterie-Division which represented XX.Armee-Korps' left flank.

On the left of the Russian columns, the 2nd and 6th divisions now thrust towards the distant villages of Michalken and Frankenau, whilst the 8th – deployed as two combat brigades – moved up to Orlau and Lahna, which Samsonov had earlier determined to be the key to the German position. If he could break their line there, he would not only be able to roll it up westwards but such a breakthrough would also uncover the route to Allenstein, thus enabling him to comply with Zhilinski's most recent instructions.

Defending the Frankenau sector was von Böckmann's 74.Infanterie-Brigade, supported by Feldartillerie-Regiment 73 and a composite regiment of infantry comprising one regular and two Landwehr infantry battalions. As he deemed this to be the most vulnerable sector of his deployment area, Scholtz also gave Böckmann the services of the corps' artillery reserve, a battalion of heavy field howitzers from Fußartillerie-Regiment 5.

Initially, everything went well for the attackers, their supporting artillery creating panic amongst the men of 70.Landwehr-Brigade – standing as a local reserve – causing it to withdraw several miles to the north. But over the next few hours, and as the range closed, the defensive fire began to take an obvious toll. It seemed as if the assault would be stopped dead in its tracks, but around 1900hrs, the Russians brought up a number of machine guns to rake the German positions. This enabled their leading elements to come within close range of the open flank of a battalion of Infanterie-Regiment 18, catastrophe only being averted when a battery of field artillery was brought up at the gallop, to pour close-range fire into the attacking columns.

With the situation balanced on a knife edge, the two Russian divisions weathered a storm of defensive fire, pushing steadily forward. Shortly before 2200hrs, with Frankenau in danger of falling, Böckmann was obliged to commit his final reserves in an attempt to shore up his position. It was a desperate but ultimately successfully manoeuvre, as the German guns hammered the enemy mercilessly. Both sides disengaged by mutual consent as darkness fell, with the lines of troops – limned by the burning buildings of Frankenau – separated in places by fewer than 500 yards.

At the other end of the 37.Infanterie-Division's sector, Wilhelmi's 73.Infanterie-Brigade would face a no less daunting challenge in the form of the Russian 8th Infantry Division.

The key to this sector lay in the villages of Orlau and Lahna, which were fated to play a similar role as Aspern and Essling a century before. Having sited his artillery to best effect, the brigade commander garrisoned each of the villages with two companies of Jäger-Bataillon 1 (Ostpreußisches) and a machine-gun company.

The action began shortly after 1400hrs when a body of Cossacks, trying to work their way around the villages, were dispersed by artillery fire. An hour later, the Russian assault began in earnest when 16 battalions of Russian infantry began their advance on Lahna, the village being held by fewer than 500 men.

Although their exact status was often questioned by other units in the army, what was never in doubt was the Jägers' marksmanship. From fortified buildings or slit trenches, a steady fire began to tear holes in the enemy formations, it naturally being claimed that few rounds – if any – missed their targets. As the attackers closed the distance, the Mauser fire was augmented by staccato bursts from the supporting Maschinengewehr (MG) 08s. Despite their grievous losses, the Russians continued forward and eventually overran the outer defences, driving ever further into the streets. Inevitably, numbers began to tell, and as the German commander Captain Bergemann fell mortally wounded, his men were increasingly forced further northwards.

At Orlau the situation was different, the village bordered to the east by woodland and to the north by the Alle River. As the first Russians came in sight, the officer in charge of the village garrison pulled his men back across the river and detonated a series of charges, destroying the bridge but abandoning the settlement to the enemy. The immediate danger thus averted, and with the enemy milling about before them, now should have been the time for the German artillery to break up the Russian advance, but a series of problems with the forward observation posts and the nature of the target area itself meant that the gunnery was at best ineffectual. This meant that whilst the threat of a direct assault had been negated, there was an ever-increasing likelihood that Russian probes along the Alle would find a point along its course where troops could be thrown across, and flank Wilhelmi's command.

The only realistic option was therefore to retake Orlau and hold it until further orders were received. The attack was scheduled for 1545hrs and was to be led by Major Weigelt and the remaining two companies of Jäger-Bataillon 1, augmented by Orlau's previous garrison, supported by two battalions of the Infanterie-Regiment 151, one each from the Infanterie-Regiment 147 together with Landwehr-Regiment 18 and a machine-gun company for fire support – some four-and-a-half battalions against a full brigade of Russian troops.

Outnumbered, it was now for the lines of green and field-grey to weather the storm of enemy fire, officers leading from the front and suffering accordingly – Major Schelle of II./Infanterie-Regiment 151 torn apart by a Russian shell as, sword in hand, he exhorted his men into the attack. His colleague Hupfeld of the 1st Battalion was likewise a victim of Russian gunnery, and Weigelt of the Jägers also fell as his men clambered over the wreckage of the bridge.

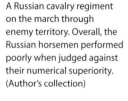

A Russian cavalry regiment on the march through enemy territory. Overall, the Russian horsemen performed poorly when judged against their numerical superiority. (Author's collection)

After an hour or so, and with their attack stalled and degenerating into chaos, many of the attacking troops simply took whatever cover they could in order to return the enemy fire. With defeat staring the Germans in the face, Wilhelmi's adjutant – Captain Appuhn – rode to Colonel Giebeler, the brigade's artillery commander, and ordered him to bring his guns forward to provide the infantry with close-in fire support.

With batteries firing over open sights at ranges of 500–600 yards, the German artillery soon forced the Russians back, before changing targets in order to silence a number of enemy batteries which had been redeployed to engage them in counter-battery fire. Sensing his moment, Wilhelmi – a conspicuous target upon a white charger – drew his sword, riding towards the sound of the fighting in an attempt to reinvigorate the attack and turn the tide.

By 1900hrs, the position had not only been successfully carried and the situation restored, but in their desperation and increasing disorganization, the troops had pursued the Russians too far. Having fought their way through waterlogged fields churned by the passage of thousands of steel-shod boots, the Germans were now in a dangerously exposed position, one that they couldn't possibly hope to hold when fighting resumed the next day.

Throughout the evening Scholtz awaited reports from the embattled sectors. When the information came, it was not good: the number of casualties aside, significant losses amongst company officers and NCOs meant that the reorganization of units would take that much longer, especially within 37.Infanterie-Division where the various units had become dangerously intermingled during the confused fighting. Any thought he may have had about renewing combat on the following morning evaporated when he received news that François' I.Armee-Korps had encountered delays during its redeployment and was not expected to be in position for joint action before noon on 26 August at the earliest.

By this time, it was clear that the 37.Infanterie-Division's position would be untenable in the face of a renewed enemy attack. After a heated discussion, Scholtz elected to 'refuse' his left flank and pull the troops back into a contiguous line between the 41.Infanterie-Division and 3.Reserve-Division, thus forming an 'inverted fish hook', with his right flank being instructed to continue improving their defensive positions. On paper this was a simple manoeuvre, but given the fractured chain of command and the close proximity to the enemy, it was – in reality – one with potential for disaster.

On the other side of the battle lines, Samsonov had reason to be satisfied. Both Orlau and Lahna had been taken, and although the former had been recaptured by the enemy, it was certain that a resumption of combat would see his XIII and XV Corps push XX.Armee-Korps aside and, by driving the enemy westwards, open the road to Allenstein.

At 0345hrs on 24 August, the Russian batteries began a bombardment preparatory to launching an attack, the random fire being largely ineffective in terms of casualties but nonetheless adding to the increasing confusion as the scattered German units made their way to safety. When his troops had reached their new positions, a battalion commander of the Infanterie-Regiment 150 would report his losses as being 106 dead, 21 wounded and 507 missing out of a theoretical strength of almost 1,100 all ranks. With their immediate objectives taken, the advancing Russians themselves halted in order to prepare for the next stage of the advance.

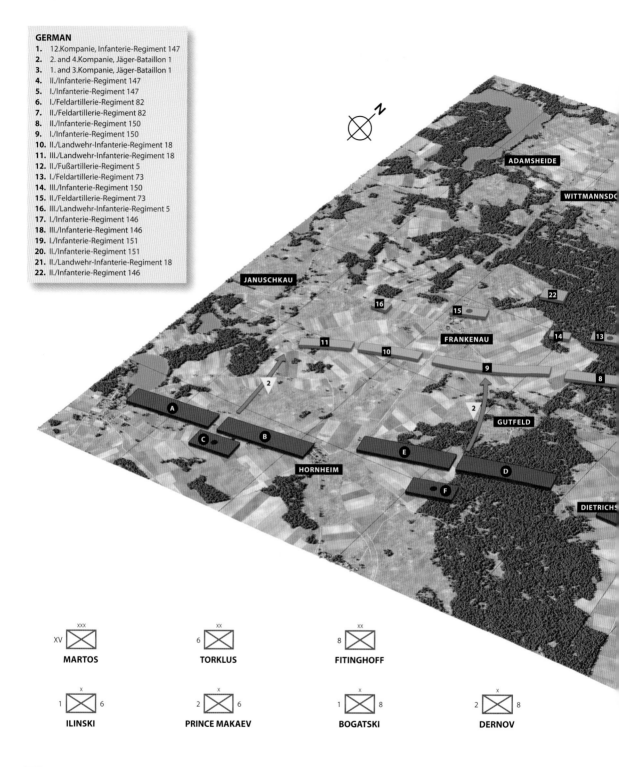

GERMAN
1. 12.Kompanie, Infanterie-Regiment 147
2. 2. and 4.Kompanie, Jäger-Bataillon 1
3. 1. and 3.Kompanie, Jäger-Bataillon 1
4. II./Infanterie-Regiment 147
5. I./Infanterie-Regiment 147
6. I./Feldartillerie-Regiment 82
7. II./Feldartillerie-Regiment 82
8. II./Infanterie-Regiment 150
9. I./Infanterie-Regiment 150
10. II./Landwehr-Infanterie-Regiment 18
11. III./Landwehr-Infanterie-Regiment 18
12. II./Fußartillerie-Regiment 5
13. I./Feldartillerie-Regiment 73
14. III./Infanterie-Regiment 150
15. III./Feldartillerie-Regiment 73
16. III./Landwehr-Infanterie-Regiment 5
17. I./Infanterie-Regiment 146
18. III./Infanterie-Regiment 146
19. I./Infanterie-Regiment 151
20. II./Infanterie-Regiment 151
21. II./Landwehr-Infanterie-Regiment 18
22. II./Infanterie-Regiment 146

ADAMSHEIDE
WITTMANNSD[...]
JANUSCHKAU
FRANKENAU
GUTFELD
HORNHEIM
DIETRICHS[...]

XV — MARTOS (XXX)
6 — TORKLUS (XX)
8 — FITINGHOFF (XX)

1 ILINSKI 6 (X)
2 PRINCE MAKAEV 6 (X)
1 BOGATSKI 8 (X)
2 DERNOV 8 (X)

EVENTS

1. Withdrawal of 12.Kompanie, Infanterie-Regiment 147 from Orlau in the face of the Russian attack.

2. Attack of the Russian 6th Infantry Division upon Michalken-Frankenau.

3. Attack of the Russian 31st and 32nd Infantry regiments upon Lahna.

4. Attack of the Russian 29th and 30th Infantry regiments upon Orlau.

5. The German counter-attacks upon Lahna and Orlau.

6. The Russian withdrawal from Lahna and Orlau.

LAHNA AND ORLAU, 23 AUGUST 1914

Shown here is the fighting around the villages of Lahna and Orlau on 23 August.

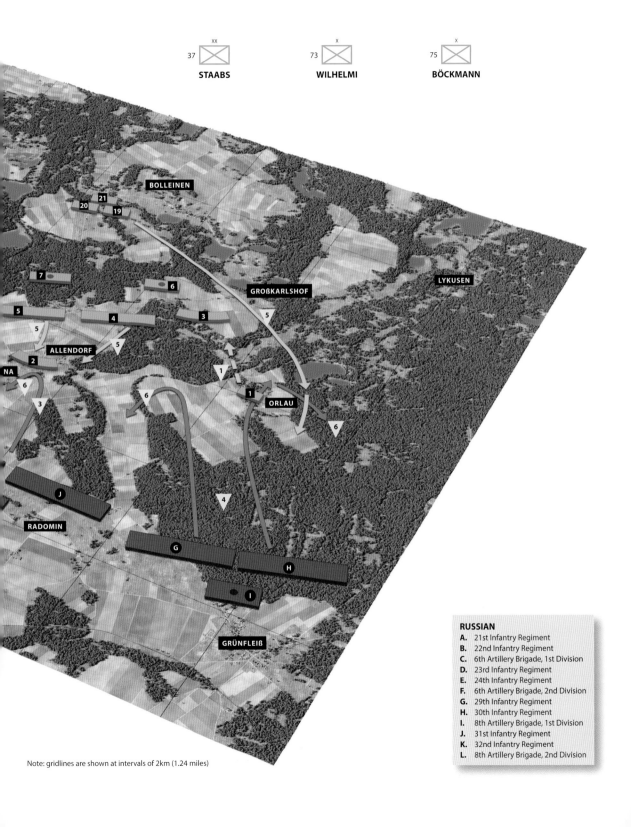

37 **STAABS** (XX)

73 **WILHELMI** (X)

75 **BÖCKMANN** (X)

BOLLEINEN

21 · 20 · 19

7 · 6

GROßKARLSHOF

LYKUSEN

5 · 4 · 3 · 5

5 · 5

ALLENDORF

2

NA

6 · 1

3 · 6 · 1

ORLAU

6

J

4

RADOMIN

G

H

I

GRÜNFLEIß

RUSSIAN
A. 21st Infantry Regiment
B. 22nd Infantry Regiment
C. 6th Artillery Brigade, 1st Division
D. 23rd Infantry Regiment
E. 24th Infantry Regiment
F. 6th Artillery Brigade, 2nd Division
G. 29th Infantry Regiment
H. 30th Infantry Regiment
I. 8th Artillery Brigade, 1st Division
J. 31st Infantry Regiment
K. 32nd Infantry Regiment
L. 8th Artillery Brigade, 2nd Division

Note: gridlines are shown at intervals of 2km (1.24 miles)

SEEING THE ELEPHANT: USDAU AND BISCHOFSBURG, 25–26 AUGUST

If his first taste of action had been unsettling for Scholtz, he was soon to be discommoded even further when he received an unannounced visit from Hindenburg and Ludendorff, who had decided to view the situation on the front line for themselves. Both men sat silent as first Scholtz and then his chief of staff outlined the events of the previous days, describing the current situation facing XX.Armee-Korps as being 'serious'. Given the inevitability of a further Russian attack in the immediate future, the corps commander suggested that whilst Unger's division remained in situ, the remainder of his troops should wheel backwards and conduct a limited withdrawal to a line Gilgenburg–Mühlen–Hohenstein, which would place his four divisions in the front line whilst the shattered 70.Landwehr-Brigade formed a general reserve. When no immediate questions were forthcoming, Scholtz continued to qualify his recommendations by adding that not only would the irregularly shaped Mühlen See act as a breakwater, funnelling any aggressive moves by the Second Army, it would also cause the enemy corps to present their flanks and rear to Mackensen and Below coming in from the north.

It was a bold suggestion to make in the face of two officers whose primary brief was to stabilize the situation on the Eastern Front, especially when it was soon clear that Scholtz was not in full possession of the facts – facts that he was soon to candidly receive.

Reassured that it was not a panic-measure, Hindenburg assented to Scholtz's suggested movement, with the proviso that – instead of remaining at Hohenstein – 3.Reserve-Division would continue moving westwards towards Reichenau, placing itself behind the line of the Drewenz River, and thus covering 37.Infanterie-Division's new positions. At this point it was Ludendorff's turn to interject: firstly, both XVII.Armee-Korps and I.Reserve-Korps had another assignment, that of observing both Rennenkampf's forces and the Russian VI Corps around Ortelsberg, and should therefore be excluded from any operational planning on Scholtz's part. Secondly, there could be no further withdrawal from the line that had just been agreed upon. If XX.Armee-Korps were to be driven north again, then François' troops would no longer be able to complete their rail transit and, if they could no longer do so, then East Prussia was almost certainly lost to the enemy. Therefore, once they had reached their new positions, Scholtz's troops must fight, hold and – if necessary – give their lives for Kaiser and Fatherland.

Returning to army headquarters, Hindenburg now made plans to visit François to gain a clear picture of I.Armee-Korps' transport situation and, assuming that things were running to schedule, make plans for its immediate deployment in support of XX.Armee-Korps. In the early hours of 25 August, and before Hindenburg and Ludendorff could set off on their journey, 8.Armee was the recipient of a stroke of luck which comes seldom in warfare. Wireless operators in Königsberg had intercepted a message between Zhilinski and Rennenkampf giving the latter firm instructions as to the next stage of his advance: he should be on a line Gerdauen–Allenburg–Wehlau before nightfall on 26 August, the message suggesting a continued enemy thrust towards Königsberg, with First Army thus moving even further away from Samsonov's forces.

As the message had been sent uncoded, it was naturally viewed with suspicion, but examples were then found of earlier messages sent 'in clear' that had been proven by subsequent events to have been accurate. If this message were indeed legitimate, and the enemy armies were diverging rather than converging, then Hindenburg held in his hands the confirmation of an unlooked-for opportunity, one which had the potential to turn the campaign on its head and restore the situation in Germany's favour.

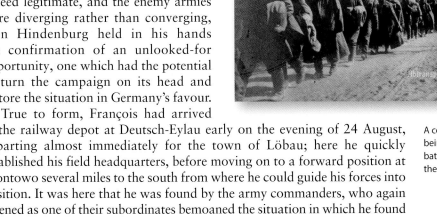

A column of Russian POWs being marched from the battlefield to holding areas in the rear. (Author's collection)

True to form, François had arrived at the railway depot at Deutsch-Eylau early on the evening of 24 August, departing almost immediately for the town of Löbau; here he quickly established his field headquarters, before moving on to a forward position at Montowo several miles to the south from where he could guide his forces into position. It was here that he was found by the army commanders, who again listened as one of their subordinates bemoaned the situation in which he found himself. This time it was not because the individual concerned had been in action, but rather because he couldn't get into action quick enough – moving away from the front line, I.Armee-Korps' movement had cut across 8.Armee's lines of supply, leading to inevitable and unavoidable delays which had been further aggravated by problems with rail facilities around Königsberg.

In a repetition of the interview with Scholtz, Hindenburg and Ludendorff remained silent whilst François listed the grounds for his corps not being in position at that time. In fact, Ludendorff was probably more aware of the actual situation than François was himself. When François was then told that at 0500hrs on 26 August, I.Armee-Korps was to attack the village of Usdau and dislodge its opposite number in the enemy order of battle, he uncharacteristically began to make excuses, stressing the parlous state of his artillery complement, both in terms of numbers and supply, especially as it would be crucial in the support of brigades whose losses in the earlier battles had yet to be fully recouped. His comments having been received by a wall of silence, François then added: 'If it is so ordered, then the attack will be made even if the men must fight with bayonets.'

His personality aside, François had quickly grasped what was still being learned on the Western Front – that a frontal attack against any prepared positions needed adequate artillery support or else it would be doomed to failure. If insufficient guns were available, then the best option would be to encourage the enemy to abandon his position by threatening his flanks. If the Russian I Corps was dug in around Usdau – he argued – this meant that it was operating defensively, as flank cover for Second Army, and its posture was therefore no direct threat to XX.Armee-Korps. A more effective option, in his respectful opinion, would be for him to ignore Usdau completely and instead strike further south, at the town of Soldau, whose capture would not only cut one of Samsonov's two supply routes but would also block the main enemy crossing point on the Neide River.

Possibly blaming François for the near disaster at Gumbinnen, Ludendorff interjected sharply: the attack would go ahead as ordered. Any probing for

After the battle Russian prisoners were subjected to manual labour before being transported west. Here POWs clear the fields under military guard. (Author's collection)

perceived enemy weaknesses would only take time, and would give that time to the enemy to react. Despite the intercepted message, if he were to hear of Samsonov experiencing extreme difficulties, Rennenkampf – no matter how unlikely – could still decide to disobey Zhilinski's orders and move to support him. A more likely outcome, however, was that Samsonov would be able to redeploy his corps to better contain this new threat and, once it had been dealt with, revert to his original plan of operations.

In a contest of wills between the two men there could only be one winner. Ludendorff icily told François that if he was unwilling to follow instructions and issue the appropriate orders for an attack, then he was free to take his place with a bayonetted rifle in the ranks of the Landser – the humble infantry – whilst another officer would be found to command the corps. Faced with such a choice, François had no option other than to confirm that he would do as ordered.

Having chastened their unruly subordinate, Hindenburg and Ludendorff told him that they were fully appreciative of his concerns and that not only would all in their power be done to ensure that I.Armee-Korps was as combat ready as possible, but that François would receive as much support as possible to ensure the success of his attack.

It was on their way back from the meeting with François that Hindenburg had his second piece of good luck in as many days. Given the fact he was often out of contact with army HQ for several hours at a time, it had become routine for regular telephone calls to be made to see if there had been any developments during the commanding general's absence. When Max Hoffmann – the Ia or principal staff officer – made such a call from Montowo, he was told that there had been a second radio interception. The core of this was that Samsonov had informed Zhilinski that XX.Armee-Korps' realignment had in fact seen a major German withdrawal along the entire front, with Zhilinski confirming that XIII, XV and XXIII Corps should continue to advance towards Allenstein, with I Corps covering their flank, whilst VI Corps moved north from Ortelsberg to counter a perceived enemy build-up in the area around Bischofsburg. If true, and again there was no reason to disbelieve its accuracy, it meant that Samsonov's Second Army would now not only be operating as three distinct entities, but more importantly, it had no immediate plans for offensive action of its own.

It was a calculated risk, based purely upon disparate pieces of captured correspondence, but one which, if it proved successful, would not only stabilize the German position in the south but would at the same time provide a springboard for further operations once Rennenkampf's intentions became clear. Satisfied that everything was going to plan, Hindenburg advised his staff that, 'our preparations are so well in hand that this evening we may all sleep soundly in our beds'.

Von Mülmann's 5.Landwehr-Brigade covered François' flank by advancing from Lautenburg towards Heinrichsdorf. The final part of the German plan was set in motion when reports received from the XX.Armee-Korps sector during the early hours of 26 August seemed to confirm a Russian movement towards Allenstein. It was clear that Scholtz's former positions between lakes Damerau and Kownatken were now only lightly defended, and could easily be carried if attacked in force. Sensing an opportunity, Ludendorff ordered Scholtz to investigate these reports further and report his findings at the earliest possible opportunity. He then went to discuss his thoughts with Hindenburg.

On the assumption that the intelligence was accurate, Ludendorff argued, it would certainly be possible for XX.Armee-Korps to overwhelm the enemy and recapture its previous positions; yet such a move would also create an opportunity to decisively support François' attack. Once the ground had been retaken, a heavily reinforced 37.Infanterie-Division would swing eastwards to face off against the now open flank of the Russian XV Corps, whilst 41.Infanterie-Division drove southwards, forcing a wedge between Usdau and Frödau whilst the enemy were frontally engaged with I.Armee-Korps, obliging them to withdraw or be captured. This would naturally require an internal redeployment of Scholtz's command, but given that François was not due to attack Usdau until early afternoon, Ludendorff felt that there would be enough time for these changes to be completed within the necessary timeframe.

At Löbau, and aware that his actions would be closely observed by Ludendorff, François issued his orders for the coming attack. At 0400hrs, 1.Infanterie-Division was to capture the enemy forward positions on the Seeben Heights, before moving upon Usdau from the north-west at 1000hrs, with 2.Infanterie-Division moving up in echelon at 0700hrs, the wheeling movement being extended by Mülmann's advance against Heinrichsdorf.

On the face of it, François was indeed obeying his orders, but nonetheless he was playing 'fast and loose' with them, being more than aware that neither of his two divisions – especially the 1st – would be in a position to comply with the agreed timings. But as the majority of his batteries had still not detrained, he was unwilling to commit his command to a frontal attack without adequate artillery support.

This inevitably meant that I.Armee-Korps' attack was delayed from the outset. When Conta later informed François that his artillery only had enough ammunition for several minutes' covering fire, the corps commander immediately requested permission to reschedule the attack to what he referred to as a more realistic timetable.

Although the request was denied, the attack on Usdau was postponed until midday, but with less than 30 minutes to go before this new deadline expired, the enemy position at Seeben had still not been carried. When army headquarters demanded to know the reasons for the delay, François snarled down the telephone that even the worst troops could hold a modern defensive line in the face of an attack by the best troops, if those attackers had insufficient artillery support.

The debris of war – Russian artillery equipment abandoned during the retreat. (Author's collection)

GERMAN
1. 1.Infanterie-Brigade
2. 2.Infanterie-Brigade
3. 3.Infanterie-Brigade
4. 4.Infanterie-Brigade
5. 5.Landwehr-Infanterie-Brigade
6. Artillery and support elements (moving by rail)
7. Gruppe Schmettau

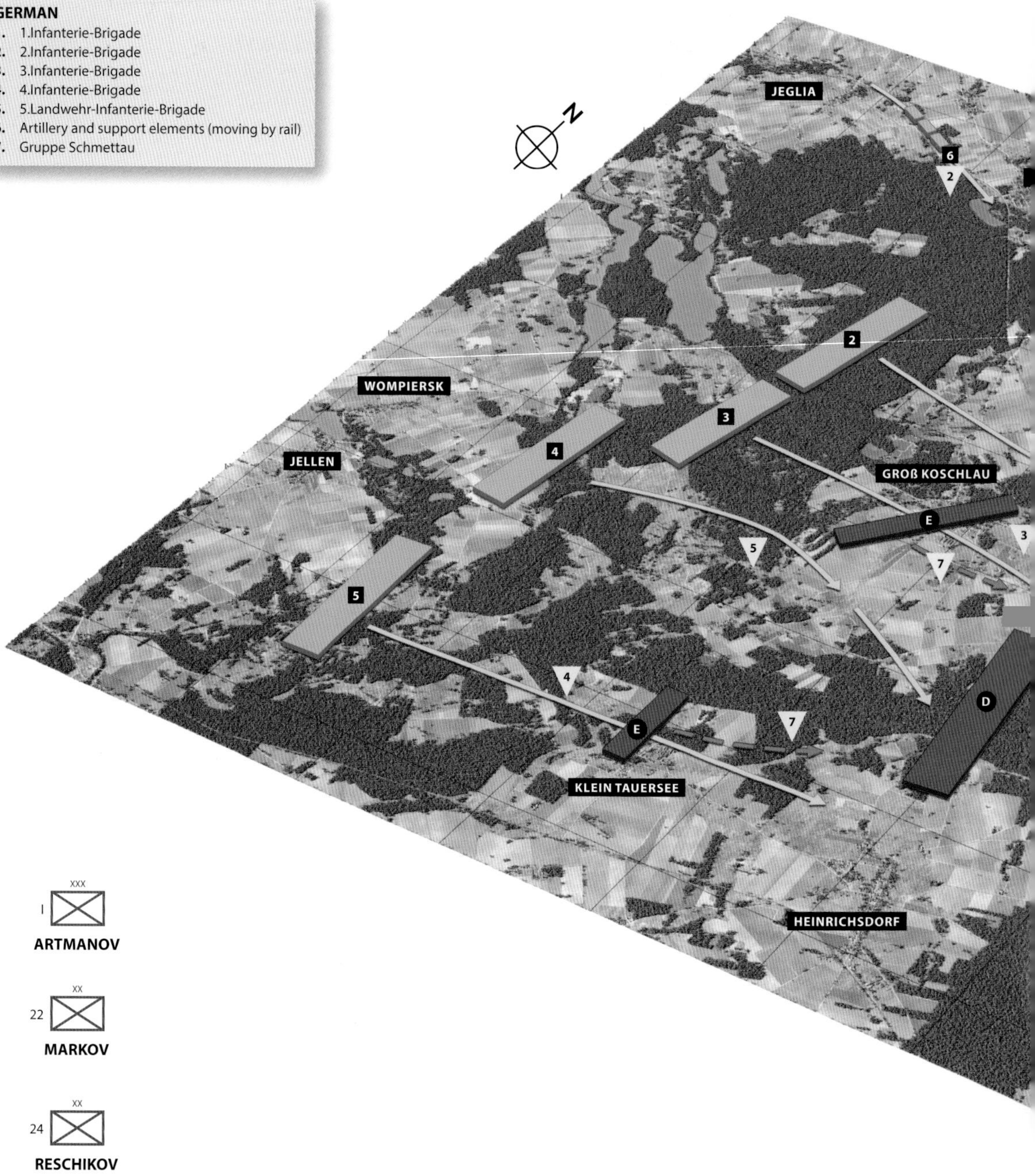

JEGLIA

WOMPIERSK

GROß KOSCHLAU

JELLEN

KLEIN TAUERSEE

HEINRICHSDORF

XXX
I ⊠
ARTMANOV

XX
22 ⊠
MARKOV

XX
24 ⊠
RESCHIKOV

▼ EVENTS

1. The German 1.Infanterie-Brigade, 1.Infanterie-Division (returning from detached service) moves into position on I.Armee-Korps' northern flank.

2. I.Armee-Korps' artillery and support elements are brought up to the front line by rail.

3. 2.Infanterie-Brigade and 3.Infanterie-Brigade move up and make a probing attack towards Groß Koschlau and Grellau.

4. 5.Landwehr-Infanterie-Brigade moves up and makes a probing attack towards Heinrichsdorf.

5. 4.Infanterie-Brigade advances parallel to event movements 3 and 4 (see above) ready to support either of them.

6. The proposed attack by elements of XX.Armee-Korps to turn the Russian positions at Usdau and Frödau in support of I.Armee-Korps' attack, indicated here, is called off as François reduces his manoeuvre to a probing attack whilst still waiting for his artillery to come up.

7. The Russian forward elements are withdrawn in the face of the German advance.

8. The Russian I Corps is redeployed to better defensive positions.

USDAU, 26 AUGUST 1914

Shown here is François' approach to the village of Usdau.

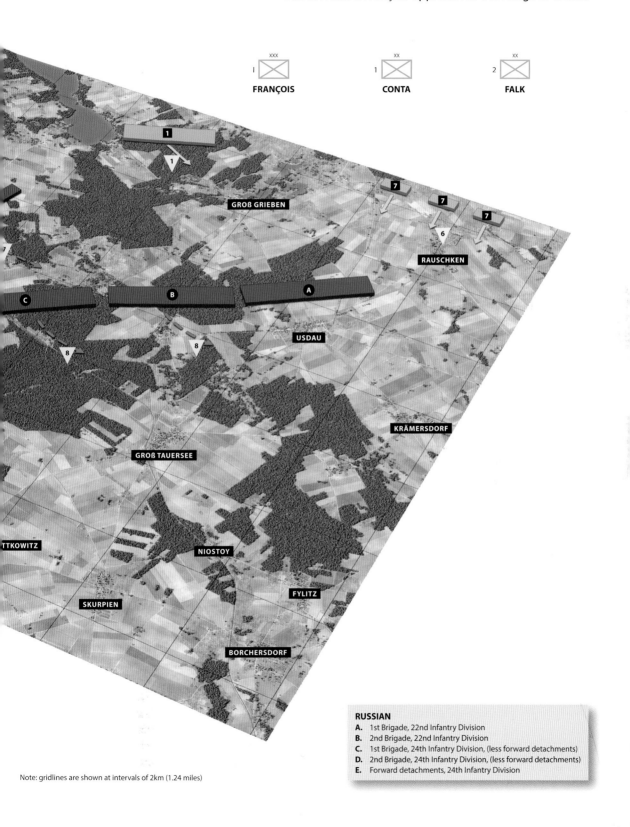

RUSSIAN
A. 1st Brigade, 22nd Infantry Division
B. 2nd Brigade, 22nd Infantry Division
C. 1st Brigade, 24th Infantry Division, (less forward detachments)
D. 2nd Brigade, 24th Infantry Division, (less forward detachments)
E. Forward detachments, 24th Infantry Division

Note: gridlines are shown at intervals of 2km (1.24 miles)

An embarrassment of riches: members of the Landsturm sorting through captured Russian equipment. (Author's collection)

This acrimonious telephone exchange continued with Ludendorff (who had mentally ruled out the option of relieving François of his command for disobeying orders) demanding to be informed the moment that I.Armee-Korps had achieved its initial objective. For his part, the corps commander continued to tinker with the timing of his attack in an effort to gain time for his artillery to arrive.

By the time that Ludendorff's deadline had expired, almost all of I.Armee-Korps was present on the battlefield, and the Seeben Heights swept clear of enemy troops with almost contemptuous ease. However, now the plan began to unravel. Conta's 1.Infanterie-Division had been marching for several hours and would need some time to reorganize and prepare for the next stage of the attack. This would mean that they would be advancing towards their objective during the hottest part of the day, with empty bellies, empty water canteens and empty ammunition pouches, all of which would hardly serve to guarantee a successful outcome. Reasoning that a failed attack would only serve to boost the enemy's morale, Conta decided to maintain his current position with a view to making a successful attack the following day, when his men had been resupplied and his artillery would be able to provide full fire support. Likewise, Falk's 2.Infanterie-Division and Mülmann's Landwehr would be able to go into action almost immediately rather than following at a distance in echelon.

No doubt relieved that the decision had effectively been taken out of his hands, and given that his other division's advance had been just as unsuccessful, François ordered the attack to be broken off at 1545hrs, informing army headquarters that he had made the decision based upon information received directly from the front line.

As this drama played itself out, Scholtz had followed Ludendorff's orders and ascertained that the troops in front of him were the men of the Russian 2nd Infantry Division. With Ludendorff having convinced Hindenburg of the potential advantages to be accrued from his proposed operation, Scholtz was given orders to redeploy XX.Armee-Korps for the attack whilst both Unger's and Morgen's divisions would hold the line of the Drewenz. Then, once the attacking divisions had secured their initial objective and begun to manoeuvre in pursuit of their secondary ones, 3.Reserve-Division would recross the river and advance upon Hohenstein to deny the enemy the major road and rail junction.

At the time when François was calling off his attack on Usdau, Scholtz was preparing to launch his own. Having softened up the enemy positions with a 15-minute bombardment, the field-grey lines began to move forward in short rushes, advancing into an increasing hail of enemy small-arms fire. Ignoring the mounting number of casualties, the German infantry pressed on again, supported by artillery batteries brought forward to give close-range fire support. The defenders' cohesion haemorrhaged when one of the attacking formations hit the gap between the two Russian brigades, the death-knell being sounded by the staccato buzz of automatic weapons when the Infanterie-Regiment 150's machine-gun company tore apart the sole Russian attempt at a counter-attack before it could be fully organized.

By 1800hrs, the trench lines had been recaptured at great cost to attackers and defenders alike. The Russian 7th (Reval) Infantry had suffered almost 3,000 casualties, and the German Infanterie-Regiment 59 had left almost 600 men lying in the wake of its advance.

This was the high-water mark of German intentions for the 26 August. With François' attack having faltered, there was no further point in Scholtz attempting to attain his secondary objectives. This decision was to be later validated by the fact that Morgen had failed to order his troops to march on Hohenstein, reasoning that to do so would place his command in the path of at least one – if not two – enemy corps, and that it would therefore be better to wait for the Russians to become engaged with XX.Armee-Korps before attempting to comply with Ludendorff's orders.

His meticulous planning rendered obsolete by the actions of others, the normally bullish Ludendorff would seem to have been overcome by a crisis of confidence, believing that François' failure to secure his objective would see the enemy massing to destroy I. and XX.Armee-Korps as fighting formations whilst Rennenkampf would likewise move to eliminate XVII.Armee-Korps and I.Reserve-Korps. Visibly shaken, he asked Hindenburg for a private conversation in order to discuss the army's situation and available options. Whilst accounts differ as to the content of the discussion, it was a noticeably calmer Ludendorff who returned, telling the assembled staff officers that the objectives for the following day would remain those that should have been taken on the 26th.

A rock of calm against the flow of his subordinate's histrionics, Hindenburg would later reflect that, 'We overcame our moment of internal crisis, we adhered to our original objectives and dedicated our every resource to their realization'.

As the operational orders for 27 August were being drafted, any cloud of despondency was dispelled by the first communication to be received from Mackensen in over 24 hours. Despite lengthy delays caused by the floods of refugees blocking the roads, he had moved his two corps towards Bischofsburg in order to engage the isolated Russian VI Corps. The latter's commander, Blagoveschensky, hampered by a series of contradictory orders from Samsonov, was now ordered to move directly on Allenstein with both his corps and the 4th Cavalry Division, leaving a detachment to hold Bischofsburg and secure his rear.

The difference between the two German corps commanders was more than noticeable. Mackensen, a fire-eater, proposed pushing his troops forward in columns of brigades to bring them into action quicker, whilst the methodical Below planned to advance in line abreast, in order to trap any enemy seeking to escape the coming battle. As a result, both formations went into action independently, not only squandering their numerical superiority, but also ensuring that Mackensen's lead elements would attack at a disadvantage.

At 0800hrs, the two forces clashed at the village of Lautern. Heineccius' 36.Infanterie-Division came to a dead halt as the call went out for the forward deployment of the divisional artillery, whilst its sister formation – the 35th – was ordered to come up on their flank. Having been roughly handled at Gumbinnen, Heineccius' men were loath to push forward, being more than content to wait it out and exchange long-range rifle fire with the enemy. Their opponents, however, had no such reluctance and began to outflank the Germans by moving into the area that by rights should already have

The scale of the Russian defeat at Tannenberg can be judged by the number of prisoners shown waiting for rail transport back to Germany. (Author's collection)

been occupied by Mackensen's second division. This potential disaster was narrowly avoided when the divisional artillery disrupted the Russian manoeuvre with a hail of shrapnel.

The question was: where was 35.Infanterie-Division? Simply put, it was still on the line of march but unable to advance further, the toll of the previous few days coupled with the summer heat having exacerbated the inevitable straggling. It would be unable to play a viable role in the developing battle until this problem had been resolved. Pessimistically, Hennig, the divisional commander, told Mackensen that it would be several hours before his command would be in position, and until then the leading elements of the corps would have to hold on as best as they could.

With Mackensen's advance 'dead in the water', Below suggested that he could salvage the situation and restore the momentum of the attack by wheeling the bulk of his command – by now including 6.Landwehr-Brigade – into the enemy rear. By 1230hrs, he had three infantry brigades in position to begin his attack, whilst his remaining brigade and the Landwehr made a diversionary attack upon the village of Groß Bößau. So far, the Germans had contrived to successfully squander every advantage they held, but their luck held out once more when Blagoveschensky, believing that he was only facing a screening force, gave orders for his 16th Division to ignore the threat and resume its march towards Allenstein.

Seeing an opportunity to strike a decisive blow against the stalled enemy column, Major-General Komarov, commander of the 4th Division, ordered his second brigade to move up and take the head of the enemy column in the flank, the quickest route taking it through Groß Bößau at almost the exact time when Below's diversionary attack began. Initially, the Russians had the better of the encounter, especially when the German reservists found themselves under fire from their own artillery in yet another incidence of 'friendly fire'. Once again, it was the willingness of individual battery commanders to bring their guns forward to the firing line that served to turn the tide. Two Landsturm batteries were brought so far forward that they actually became the spearhead of the German attack, effectively obliging the infantry to advance in their support.

By this stage fully aware that something was exceptionally amiss in the Bischofsburg sector, Blagoveschensky countermanded the 16th Division's orders, commanding it to return to Bischofsburg. With the regimental columns strung out along the road, the troops complied as best they could, but in the obvious confusion, basic elements of security were neglected and the khaki-clad infantry unknowingly found themselves marching across the front of the enemy's 1.Reserve-Division, en route to support Mackensen's beleaguered troops.

Disaster struck with a reverberating clap of thunder as the Russians found themselves taken in the flank by massed German artillery firing over open sights, sweeping them from the field and from the battle.

By 1700hrs, Mackensen's troops had finally completed their reorganization and were now able to take the battle to the Russian 4th Division. The latter's single remaining brigade cracked under the overwhelming pressure, completing the rout of Blagoveschensky's corps, which fell back with the loss of around 5,000 men.

With numerical superiority, Mackensen's plan had obviously been the correct one, but it should be noted that by signally failing to take notice of the condition of the men of his own corps, let alone those of his supporting units, he was compromising his own orders even as he issued them. What saved him from defeat was the series of even more contradictory orders issued by both Samsonov and Blagoveschensky, coupled with their complete misreading of the tactical situation around Bischofsburg. This meant that the forces already there were far too dispersed to be committed effectively, and by the time that Komarov had decided to combine his brigades to attack Mackensen's spearhead, his men were already outnumbered over four to one.

Despite the hard-fought victory, both German commanders knew that they were not 'out of the woods'. One enemy corps had been roughly handled, it was true, but their most recent intelligence reports stated that there were a further two within striking distance somewhere to the north-east and a further three to their front. Unknowingly aided by a 'funk' into which Blagoveschensky had fallen – he would wait until late the following afternoon before informing Samsonov that there had even been a battle at Bischofsburg, let alone that he had been heavily defeated and was therefore retreating in disorder rather than advancing as instructed – Mackensen opted for the cavalryman's tactic and pressed on regardless.

The chess pieces were slowly moving into place, and with his personal morale restored, Ludendorff now issued the decisive orders for 27 August. The objective was the destruction of the Russian XV Corps, together with those elements of the XXIII Corps that had been roughly handled by Scholtz's troops earlier that afternoon. To that end, François – supported by 5.Landwehr-Brigade – was to resume his attack upon Usdau, whilst Scholtz, having detached several battalions to make a subsidiary attack between Usdau and Frödau, was to continue pushing into the flank of the enemy's XV and XXIII Corps; meanwhile, Morgen and Unger would consolidate a defensive line from Hohenstein to the Mühlen See.

As an operation it lacked tactical finesse; instead, the enemy edifice should be hammered by successive attacks until it cracked and then, when it did, the fault line was to be exploited with all available force.

Russian POWs in a railway carriage. A total of 60 trains were required to transport the prisoners back to Germany. (Author's collection)

With the evening of 26 August drawing to a close, there was one more moment of drama when Morgen, upon receipt of his orders, belatedly informed Ludendorff that he was not actually in possession of Hohenstein, having remained in his original position in anticipation of an enemy attack that had never materialized. Luckily for Morgen, Scholtz stepped in and defused the potential pyrotechnics by informing both Hindenburg and Ludendorff that he would feel more comfortable in executing their instructions if he knew that Morgen and Unger were covering his left flank rather than being extended far to the north. Once more, the army high command deferred to the knowledge of the 'man on the spot'.

THE SOUND OF THE GUNS: USDAU, 27 AUGUST

For Hermann von François, this was to be the moment of truth. To date, his campaign record had been a catalogue of underachievement. The engagement at Stallupönen had been unsuccessful, his role in the commitment of the bulk of the 8.Armee at Gumbinnen had almost led to disaster and just the day before he had singularly failed to secure his objective. But now, all of the reasons, all of the excuses that he had given for the failed attempt on Usdau had lost any validity: his men were rested and resupplied, his artillery complement was present and ready for action. The only options were victory or a heroic death, and he had no intention of emulating his father, who had fallen at Spicheren in 1870.

At 0400hrs, I.Armee-Korps' artillery would begin a bombardment of the Russian positions, the guns maintaining their fire when the infantry stepped off an hour later and only slackening when the guns overheated, needed resupply or when the attacking lines became too close to their objective so as to differentiate friend from foe. At this point, the batteries would receive further fire missions as dictated by the developing situation.

With Conta moving on Usdau from the north-west, Falk's 4.Infanterie-Brigade would attack the town from the south with his 3.Infanterie-Brigade acting as flank cover. Further security would be provided by 5.Landwehr-Brigade moving forward from Heinrichsdorf, the intent being that the infantry would be in their assault positions as the sun rose, ready to launch their attack as the artillery moved onto its secondary targets.

Having consolidated their position and advanced some distance closer to Usdau during the course of the previous evening, Falk's men would end up going into action first with the 3.Infanterie-Brigade moving on Groß Tauersee. Meanwhile, 4.Infanterie-Brigade was to take Meischitz and then bypass Usdau, occupying the high ground to the south of the town, thereby blocking the enemy's natural line of retreat. One and a quarter miles from their objectives, the men of 2.Infanterie-Division began to come under fire from the Russian positions, its volume increasing when, with the sun rising and visibility improving, the Russian artillery began to join in.

To the north, and seeing his role as being more that of a blocking force than that of an assault column, Bernhard Böß, in command of Falk's 4.Infanterie-Brigade, merely kept his head down, moving further and further east, aiming to draw as little attention to his command as possible in order to reach his objective with minimal unnecessary loss. Accordingly, and having seen little or no action, 4.Infanterie-Brigade secured the high ground east of Meischitz at around 1115hrs.

As the artillery bombardment continued, Conta's staff officers waited anxiously as the seconds ticked towards and then past the 'jump-off point' of 0500hrs, their chief allowing the gunners – reinforced by artillery detached from the garrison of Thorn – to soften up their targets even further. Eventually, the divisional commander signalled his assent, and orders went down the line for the troops to advance, hopefully under cover of a continuous barrage. Although the attack went smoothly, it was not without incident as there were further – seemingly by now routine – examples of the German gunners dropping shells into the ranks of their own men.

Shortly before 1100hrs, the first German infantry entered the outskirts of the by-now burning village, only to find that its sole occupants were either dead or dying. As the weight of the German bombardment intensified, and when it became clear that the enemy were in the process of cutting the Usdau–Soldau road, a number of battery commanders took it upon themselves to 'save' their precious guns rather than risk their loss. As they did so, so did many of the infantry, those who had not already made their minds to surrender. With the national colours being run up to signal the change in possession, Conta sent a runner to François' headquarters to confirm that his objectives had been attained.

His jubilation tempered by the lacklustre performance of Falk's division, François called Ludendorff in person to deliver the news of his success, requesting permission to realign the thrust of his advance in the direction of Soldau, in order to both consolidate his position and to prevent the enemy commander from making any attempt to rally his troops. Hindenburg signalled his assent to the request, and François began to draft orders for this new phase in the battle. His intent was to completely sever the enemy's line of retreat by establishing a strong position on the northern bank of the Neide before turning eastwards and attacking into the soft underbelly of the Russian Second Army. With the news of François' victory, Hindenburg and Ludendorff decided to reduce the headquarters at Löbau, and set up a field headquarters closer to the front, from where they could better react to the fluid situation. For the next hour or two, they would be dangerously out of direct contact with both of their corps commanders.

Ostensibly, Artmanov's position based on the line Soldau–Usdau–Frödau had been a strong one: his men had had adequate time to entrench and fortify their positions, whilst his artillery was well sited in prepared positions calculated to take a toll on any attacking forces. However, even such strength was a weakness if not supported by other disciplines. The Russian I Corps had two independent cavalry divisions at its disposal, comprising eight regiments of cavalry with attendant horse artillery. But instead of being deployed to find and observe the enemy, they were merely used for flank security – and only one flank at that – Artmanov seemingly being content to leave the security of his right flank to the 2nd Division which, in any event, had already been swept aside by XX.Armee-Korps a day earlier. That, combined with the scale of the enemy bombardment and the receipt of a series of increasingly contradictory orders, had created an environment which quickly turned a possible withdrawal into a rout, a total collapse ensuing when the artillery around Usdau began to pull back.

Having ordered the retreat, Artmanov now had only two real choices available to him. The first and undoubtedly the best of these would have been to retire eastwards in order to unite with the remainder of the army, preserving his strength for combat in the days ahead. Instead, he chose the second option and withdrew towards Soldau, increasing the distance between himself and the rest of the army, mirroring Blagoveschensky's earlier achievement. Both commanders' failures effectively negated Samsonov's numerical advantage by reducing the forces available to him to a force of roughly two and a half corps – none of which was by now at full strength.

TURNING THE FLANK: 27 AUGUST

Although happy that his left flank was secure, Scholtz had been vocally sceptical on the evening of 26 August when he found that his new orders

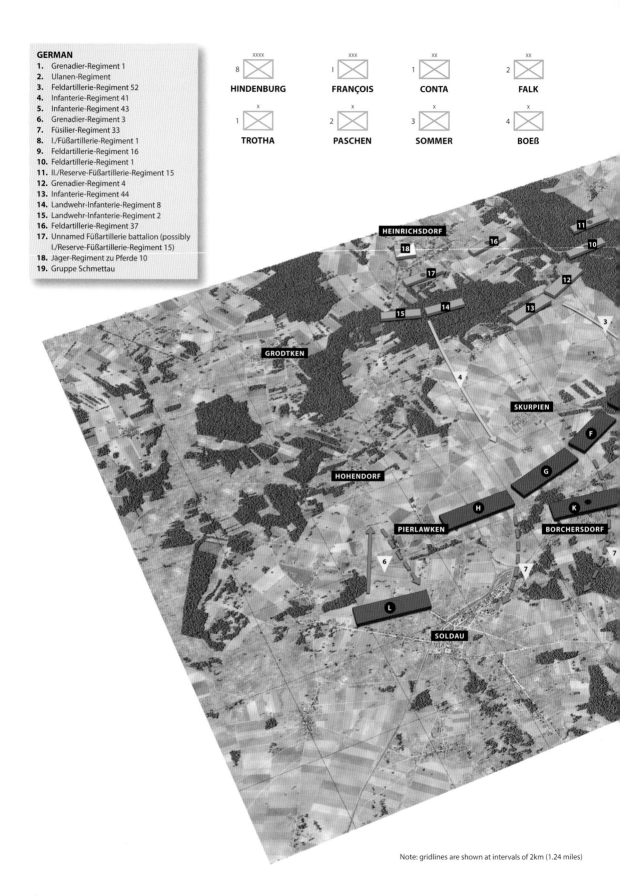

GERMAN

1. Grenadier-Regiment 1
2. Ulanen-Regiment
3. Feldartillerie-Regiment 52
4. Infanterie-Regiment 41
5. Infanterie-Regiment 43
6. Grenadier-Regiment 3
7. Füsilier-Regiment 33
8. I./Füßartillerie-Regiment 1
9. Feldartillerie-Regiment 16
10. Feldartillerie-Regiment 1
11. II./Reserve-Füßartillerie-Regiment 15
12. Grenadier-Regiment 4
13. Infanterie-Regiment 44
14. Landwehr-Infanterie-Regiment 8
15. Landwehr-Infanterie-Regiment 2
16. Feldartillerie-Regiment 37
17. Unnamed Füßartillerie battalion (possibly
    I./Reserve-Füßartillerie-Regiment 15)
18. Jäger-Regiment zu Pferde 10
19. Gruppe Schmettau

HINDENBURG — FRANÇOIS — CONTA — FALK

TROTHA — PASCHEN — SOMMER — BOEß

Note: gridlines are shown at intervals of 2km (1.24 miles)

USDAU, AFTERNOON, 27 AUGUST 1914

Shown here are the events at Usdau on the afternoon of 27 August.

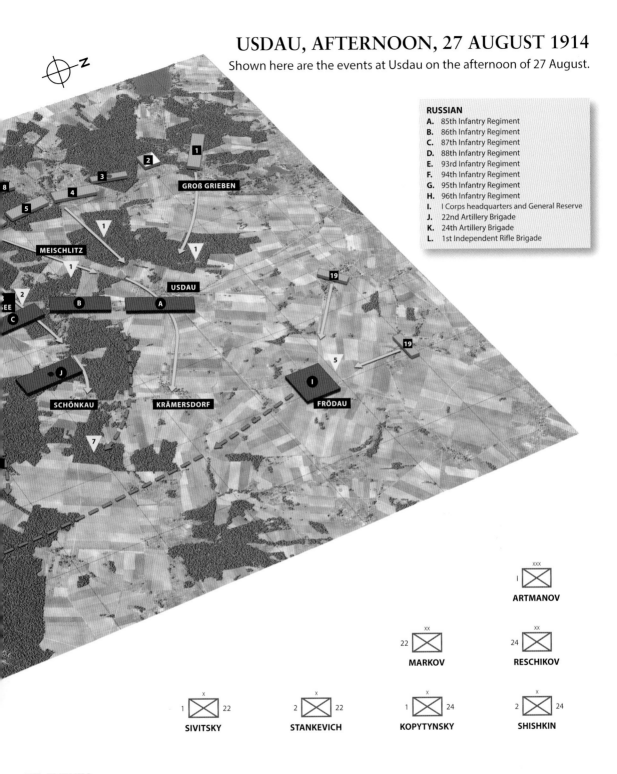

RUSSIAN
- **A.** 85th Infantry Regiment
- **B.** 86th Infantry Regiment
- **C.** 87th Infantry Regiment
- **D.** 88th Infantry Regiment
- **E.** 93rd Infantry Regiment
- **F.** 94th Infantry Regiment
- **G.** 95th Infantry Regiment
- **H.** 96th Infantry Regiment
- **I.** I Corps headquarters and General Reserve
- **J.** 22nd Artillery Brigade
- **K.** 24th Artillery Brigade
- **L.** 1st Independent Rifle Brigade

I — ARTMANOV

22 — MARKOV

24 — RESCHIKOV

1 / 22 — SIVITSKY

2 / 22 — STANKEVICH

1 / 24 — KOPYTYNSKY

2 / 24 — SHISHKIN

EVENTS

1. German advance upon Usdau and then Krämersdorf.
2. German advance upon Groß Tauersee and then Schönkau.
3. German advance upon Groß Tauersee and then Borchersdorf.
4. German advance upon Skurpien.
5. Flank move against Frödau by elements of XX.Armee-Korps.
6. Attack (and withdrawal) of 1st Independent Rifle Brigade towards Hohendorf.
7. Withdrawal of I Corps towards Soldau.

effectively specified a synchronization between I. and XX.Armee-Korps. Still fuming at what he perceived as François' dilettante attitude to the conduct of war and the chain of command, he complained directly to Ludendorff, stressing that it was only by chance that his colleague's signal failure of the preceding day had not caused his own troops to suffer a serious reverse.

Somewhat mollified by the response he received, Scholtz began to issue his own orders for the following day. Firstly, and in some way to exculpate himself for his recent inaction, Morgen's 3.Reserve-Division was to make a diversion towards Hohenstein, which – Scholtz hoped – would draw the enemy to him. This would allow 37. and 41.Infanterie-Division – less a force that would be detached to support François' attack on Usdau – to strike the Russian XV and XXIII corps as they reacted to Morgen's movement in the north.

With 73.Infanterie-Brigade of Staabs' 37.Infanterie-Division having been weakened to provide the core of the force being sent to François' assistance and kept as a local reserve, Scholtz was able to commit three brigades for the coming operation – Staabs' remaining brigade (the 75th) and both brigades of Sontag's 41.Infanterie-Division, together with the corps assets, a force in the region of 14,000 men.

Initial progress was slow, the men undoubtedly remembering the chaos of the previous day and fearing that they could become embroiled in an enemy counter-attack at any moment. Yard by yard, minute by minute, they advanced, the silence punctuated by isolated bursts of fire that slowly died down until, at around 0900hrs, the three brigades halted in preparation to repel the inevitable enemy counter-attack that many felt was forming up just out of sight.

Their waiting would be in vain, as there were literally no Russians to their front or, for that matter, to their flanks. The troops with whom they had been skirmishing had been the remnants of the Russian 2nd Division, against whom they had fought the previous day. These Russians, by now hungry and low on ammunition, had simply broken in disorder, their precipitate flight easily outdistancing the cautious German advance.

The game of chess has its origins in the depiction of a field of battle, but it goes without saying that in real life events move simultaneously. Thus, whilst Hindenburg was busily calming his distraught subordinate, and whilst both Scholtz and François were making their plans for 27 August, Klujew and Martos – commanding the Russian XIII and XV corps respectively – were already in the process of executing theirs, with Klujew continuing to push north through the Allensteiner Forst, while Martos had turned his attention to the German forces deployed along the Drewenz. At 0430hrs, his massed artillery began a concentrated bombardment of the German positions around Mühlen. This led to extreme consternation at Scholtz's headquarters when a radio intercept around midday confirmed Samsonov's orders for Martos to launch an attack in that sector. Horrified, Scholtz was hit by the icy realization that whilst his most effective units were 'off station' in an attempt to find and engage the enemy rear, the enemy was within striking distance of his own; his only defence comprised two second-line formations, one of whose commanders had recently been unwilling to obey orders that he disagreed with. If these weren't grounds enough for concern, the location of a second enemy corps was still unknown and it could even now be preparing to roll up his lines whilst Martos' attack fixed his forces in position.

The nascent panic only increased when Scholz, attempting to personally report to Hindenburg, was told that both the army commander and his deputy were in the process of establishing a new forward headquarters and that it could be some time before secure communications were established. Eventually, the two men spoke, with Hindenburg listening politely and opining that in every difficulty lies opportunity. He directed Scholtz to contain this new threat by moving XX.Armee-Korps around the southern edge of the Mühlen See to threaten Martos' lines of communication by occupying the village of Waplitz.

The operation foundered almost as soon as it was ordered, with reports coming in that the German line had been broken to the north of Mühlen and that the enemy were pouring into the gap. The 73.Infanterie-Brigade was immediately ordered to the threatened sector, to be followed by the remainder of Staabs' division as soon as it could be redeployed. Sontag was therefore directed to conduct the attack with his single division. By 1700hrs, only having made it as far as Januschkow on the southern shore of the Mühlen See, Sontag simply ordered his men to halt and dig in.

North of Mühlen, it transpired that the reports of the enemy breakthrough had been grossly exaggerated, the catalyst being a unit that had broken under Russian artillery fire. Indeed, the confused fighting in the sector had redounded heavily to the defenders' favour when almost 1,000 Russian infantry, having taken part in a failed attack, had simply elected to surrender rather than risk retreating through the hail of small-arms and artillery fire coming from both sides. With Morgen holding the left of the line, and Sontag the right, Scholtz was now relatively secure.

As Martos threw himself against XX.Armee-Korps, the only Russian formation yet to engage was Klujew's XIII Corps, and like his compatriots he was soon to be overtaken by a combination of unanticipated events and contradictory orders. Ostensibly, the corps was to cooperate with Blagoveschensky in the capture of Allenstein, after which – having garrisoned the town – both units were to support XV Corps' turning movement.

Hearing the sound of the firing near Mühlen, Klujew conscientiously contacted Samsonov's headquarters to ask for instructions, and was told to continue his march on Allenstein. Attempts to communicate with VI Corps in order to work out a common plan for the capture of the rail hub collapsed when the reply was found to be in a cipher for which XIII Corps did not possess the key. Unable to talk to either of the men who could clarify the situation for him, Klujew elected to ignore a request for help he had received from Martos, choosing instead to follow the last instructions he had been given, his adherence to orders no doubt being influenced by the presence of the German supply depot at Allenstein.

INTERLUDE AT OSTERODE

With events literally hanging on a knife edge, both Hindenburg and Ludendorff were of the opinion that Löbau had outlived its suitability as army headquarters, and that a new one should be established closer to the front line. Although this would increase the risk, it would naturally improve communications with the troops in the field. Accordingly, the town of Osterode was chosen for the new headquarters. Oberleutnant von Stephani of the staff was sent ahead with the dual mission of choosing a suitable building to house the army staff, and then

Abandoned Russian trenches.
(Author's collection)

to travel on to Allenstein to discuss the arrival of a Landwehr division which was in the process of being transferred from Schleswig, which Hindenburg desired to detrain as close to the fighting as possible so as to enable its immediate deployment for action.

Osterode, like many towns, was filled to overflowing with refugees from the eastern part of the province, and it took Stephani some time to complete the first part of his assignment, before heading to the railway station to commandeer a locomotive for the journey to Allenstein. In this he was also successful, but due to limited facilities the engine was obliged to travel in reverse; as they approached their destination, one of the engine crew pointed out what looked like a number of troops milling around the railway station. Stephani laughed this off adding that they were undoubtedly more refugees making their way west.

Later unable to explain why, at some stage Stephani took out his field glasses to study the 'refugees', only to discover that the supposed civilians were in fact Russian infantry sitting down to their midday meal. Slowing down, but needing to come to a full stop before it could reverse its course, the engine glided agonizingly towards the station, with more and more khaki-clad troops looking up incredulously from their food at the grey-uniformed figure standing in the engine house staring back at them, pistol in hand.

For long moments the tableau remained frozen, but then, as the wheels finally came to a halt, it was shattered by the sound of bullets ricocheting from steel plate. Releasing the brakes, the driver frantically reversed gears, and as the men in the cabin took what cover they could from the Russian fire, the engine gradually gathered speed, taking agonizing moments to leave the station and pull away from the enemy troops.

The confirmation that Allenstein was in enemy hands resulted in three significant alterations to the German plan. Firstly, von der Goltz's Landwehr division from Schleswig would now detrain at Biesellen on the Passarge to cover the approaches to Osterode. Secondly, Scholtz opted to place 37.Infanterie-Division on the flank of Morgen's 3.Reserve-Division. Thirdly, and perhaps most important of all, Mackensen's two corps, which had been conducting mopping-up operations in the Bischofsburg area before moving on Passenheim, now had a new objective.

A DAY OF DECISION: 28 AUGUST

Lieutenant von Stephani's rude awakening as he steamed into Allenstein would ultimately be the cause of another ripple of indecision at army headquarters, as the presence of enemy troops within striking distance of the German rear naturally engendered several questions, all of which needed to be resolved with the utmost dispatch.

Whose troops had Stephani seen? Had Rennenkampf finally come to his colleague's aid? Was this part of an overall strategy by Second Army, or had

Samsonov fatally overextended himself? Whatever the answers, there was but one certainty: whichever course of action 8.Armee chose to pursue, it would be undertaken by XVII.Armee-Korps and I.Reserve-Korps.

The German staff officers began collating reports on the evening of the 27th. The previous days' fighting had accounted for at least two enemy corps being driven back in disorder – and thus they posed no immediate threat – and Martos' XV Corps was engaged with Scholtz's troops. Thus, there could be no more than a single Russian corps in Allenstein.

With their corps still in the process of re-establishing contact with headquarters, it fell to Below – who spoke to Ludendorff first – to suggest that the logical step would be to launch an attack on Allenstein, driving the enemy forces there southwards onto Scholtz's guns.

The merit of such a plan was easily perceived, not merely because it would both stabilize the situation and provide a much-needed fillip with the liberation of the town, but just as importantly the enforced compression of the enemy forces would cause Martos significant difficulties in continuing his attacks on the XX.Armee-Korps sector. Agreeing to Below's suggestion, Ludendorff consented to a joint – but not necessarily coordinated – attack, which needed to be underway by midday on 28 August. The latter codicil was added to ensure that, irrespective of Mackensen's situation, Below's men would be in position to attack at the appointed time. Being informed that XVII.Armee-Korps had still to contact army headquarters, Below offered to send his chief of staff – Colonel Posadowsky – to brief Mackensen in person. The next day, Ludendorff stressed, was to be a 'day of decision'.

In the meantime, XVII.Armee-Korps' communications had been fully restored, and a series of differing, and in some cases contradictory, orders had been received from army HQ. In such circumstances, the plan almost fell apart before it had been implemented, but being personally acquainted with I.Reserve-Korps' chief of staff, Mackensen was prepared to suppress any concerns he was entertaining and to fully commit his troops to the proposed attack.

Elsewhere, events had also been shifting in the Germans' favour when Martos, committed to the fighting along the Drewenz, requested that Klujew's XIII Corps be released to support his attack – only to be told that Samsonov expected him to disengage and – on the 28th – march in support of the corps occupying Allenstein (a situation that would naturally become moot when the outcome of the fighting at Bischofsburg finally became known). Refusing point-blank to countenance such an action in the face of an undefeated enemy, Martos demanded to be relieved of command and threatened to resign his commission on the spot.

Whether frustration or outright bluff, Martos' outburst had the desired effect, with Second Army's commander showing just how far removed his appreciation of the tactical situation was from its reality. Samsonov thus relented and granted the petition, stating that whilst Klujew's corps moved to support Martos, Blagoveschensky's VI Corps would continue to consolidate the Russian position around Allenstein and Passenheim. It was at this moment, with the junction of the two corps being 'covered' by a non-existent one, that Samsonov ensured his own defeat, his orders effectively creating the situation that would lead to the encirclement of the bulk of his command. But fate had not yet finished with the Russian commander. On the morning of 28 August, and by now fully aware of the defeats suffered by both of his flanking formations, he personally informed Zhilinski that he would be moving his headquarters into the field to oversee the joint actions by XIII and XV corps – in hindsight, this was doubtless preparation for the terrestrial equivalent of a captain going down with his ship.

On the western bank of the Drewenz, Scholtz, stung by Hindenburg's previous criticism, and believing that he had found a gap in the Russian lines, decided to take the initiative. Sontag's 41.Infanterie-Division was ordered to advance around the southern part of the Mühlen See and occupy the village of Paulsgut. Once this objective was secured, Morgen and Unger would launch a general attack to their front, with 37.Infanterie-Division moving in support. The attack began as scheduled, at 0400hrs, but with visibility impaired by heavy fog, progress was tortuously slow. As the troops passed through the abandoned hamlet of Adamsheide, the silence was shattered by the local rooster challenging the shadowy figures. With the local Russian forces thus alerted to their danger, men began moving and firing in all directions, unsure and unaware of exactly where friend and foe were to be found. As the sun rose and the fog dissipated, Sontag's men found themselves targeted by several enemy batteries, which, firing to great effect, brought the German advance to a dead halt.

Within a short time, what had begun as a penetration of the enemy line had become reduced to a pocket, one which collapsed under the weight of unchallenged Russian artillery fire, as again the German gunners failed to adequately support their comrades in the infantry. The principal achievement of the German artillery at this time was the shelling of Waplitz, whose capture by friendly troops could not be capitalized upon due to the bombardment and, in time, the bulk of the small garrison would march into Russian captivity.

As casualties mounted, the men of 35.Feldartillerie-Regiment dramatically retrieved their honour by moving out of cover and deploying in the open to engage the Russians over open sights, sacrificing themselves in order to cover the division's retreat. In less than three hours, Sontag's 41.Infanterie-Division had lost almost 2,500 men.

His plan unravelling, Scholtz was less than enthusiastic when he discovered that – having come to judge the situation for themselves – Hindenburg and Ludendorff had arrived at Frögenau, just behind the front line. They immediately began firing off a barrage of questions that demanded immediate answers – but an even more urgent one was soon on everyone's lips when a radio intercept suggested that Klujew planned to link up with Martos by lunchtime on the 28th.

Reeling from these latest developments, Scholtz now received a message that offered a modicum of comfort. Despite there being no signal indicating the success of Sontag's flanking manoeuvre, the commanding officer of 3.Reserve-Division, Kurt von Morgen – who had earlier shown a facility for disobeying orders that he didn't agree with – had decided to order an attack on his own initiative. At 0730hrs, under cover of an artillery barrage, three of Morgen's four brigades had launched a frontal attack on the enemy before them, whilst the fourth, 6.Landwehr-Brigade, moved through the forested terrain to its front in order to find and turn the enemy's flank.

Ambition soon succumbed to reality as the German second- and third-tier troops advanced into a storm of enemy fire, their ranks flensed by an unseen enemy firing from concealment. As the casualty list increased, the sole light of hope shone from 6.Landwehr-Brigade, whose commander Adolf Krahmer used his machine-gun companies to suppress the enemy positions whilst the infantry advanced in textbook rushes. Inch by inch, and yard by yard, Krahmer's men forced their way until they finally reached the outskirts of Hohenstein, several hours after they had first begun their advance.

To the north, and as the battle raged, Goltz's division was in the process of assembling at Biesellen before taking up position on Scholtz's left. Leaving the remainder of his command to follow once they had detrained, Goltz set off with a force of seven battalions, almost half of his strength, heading towards Hohenstein – and inadvertently marched straight into the leading elements of the Russian XIII Corps, which was moving westwards from Allenstein.

Deploying from march column, the Landwehr formed up for the attack under sustained enemy fire, their officers falling as they sought to lead their men from the front. All of a sudden, the Russian fire slackened off, becoming visibly more sporadic as the defending troops began to decamp in the face of a line of field-grey troops emerging towards their rear – elements of Krahmer's 6.Landwehr-Brigade moving past the outskirts of Hohenstein.

Ludendorff's 'day of decision' was not going as he had hoped or anticipated: all three commanders – Morgen, Goltz and Sontag – had been halted, and XX.Armee-Korps was now facing far more enemy troops than had originally been anticipated. The only immediate good news was derived from inference rather than by gathered intelligence or hard fact: if the Russian XIII Corps was confirmed as moving up in support of Martos' XV Corps, it stood to reason that the movement against Allenstein had been successful and thus Mackensen and Below were now within supporting distance. Ironically, it would be Ludendorff's *bête noire* François who would in fact salvage the situation.

Whilst preparing for his proposed attack on Soldau, the commander of I.Armee-Korps had consolidated all of his available artillery, roughly 120 guns, with the task of breaking the enemy before the infantry attacked. Their task would be made simpler by the exclusive allocation of his aerial elements to the reconnaissance of the enemy positions and planning of indirect fire solutions. It was one of these aerial sorties which indicated that, instead of preparing to defend the river crossing at Soldau, the enemy were pulling even further back, and that the town would be there for the taking if a determined thrust were made.

Early on the 28th, with opportunity staring him in the face and aware that to occupy Soldau with his entire force would be a waste of resources, François sent a flying column under Oberstleutnant Schäffer von Berstein to both cut the Neidenburg road and conduct a reconnaissance in force to the north-east whilst the main body moved against Soldau. He only had the vaguest information on what was happening in XX.Armee-Korps' sector, but anticipated that if any Russians were to move on his position – under whatever circumstance or condition – then this would be the route that they would use.

At 0600hrs, the massed batteries opened fire, raining destruction upon their target as the infantry prepared to advance. But before the guns fell silent, François made a final change to his plan, deciding to pull Falk's 2.Infanterie-Division out of the battle line in anticipation of the first positive reports from the direction of Neidenburg.

With his troops under sporadic fire, and with aircraft now patrolling the skies between Soldau and Mlawa, it was becoming increasingly obvious to

François that the Russian defence was nothing more than an empty shell. He immediately ordered 2.Infanterie-Division to follow the flying column and occupy Neidenburg, there to await further instructions.

Naturally relieved at some tangible success having been derived from the day's operations, Hindenburg and Ludendorff felt even more so when a study of the map showed how close Neidenburg was to the threatened 41.Infanterie-Division. Back to his usual self, Ludendorff telephoned François and, in the army commander's name, instructed him to redeploy both 2.Infanterie-Division and the XX.Armee-Korps detachment to the Mühlen See with orders to turn back the enemy attack and stabilize the situation. Before ending the call, Ludendorff instructed François to telephone army headquarters in person once the orders had been given and the troops were underway.

With the prevalence of modern communications meaning that a commander was – in theory at least – never out of contact with his troops, concerning messages were being received by 8.Armee headquarters at an alarming rate, each reporting an increasingly pessimistic view of the German position. No sooner had he confirmed Falk's new orders than François was instructed to leave a reasonable force at Soldau – 5.Landwehr-Brigade – to dig in and put the town in a state of defence whilst consolidating the remainder of his command around Lahna and Orlau, prior to receiving updated instructions upon arrival. For the bullish general, deploying an army corps to cover the retreat of a single division was far too excessive. With the courage of conceit he ordered Conta to come off the line of march to rest and feed his troops, creating a much-needed reserve in the event of his corps coming into combat in the adverse terrain between their current position and new objective. It was a potentially dangerous move to contemplate, but with his unspoken motto *l'audace, encore de l'audace, toujours de l'audace!* (We must dare, dare again, and go on daring!), François naturally thought that he had a far better appreciation of the realities of the situation than any other officer in the army. In any event, he reasoned to himself that with Soldau and eventually Neidenburg in German hands, the enemy would soon have far more pressing concerns than the destruction of Sontag's beleaguered command.

THE BEGINNINGS OF COLLAPSE: 28–29 AUGUST

Throughout the afternoon, reports flowed into 8.Armee headquarters from every formation on the front line. In the end only one of these mattered: Sontag's position had stabilized considerably, and there was no sign of an enemy pursuit. As such, he was reorganizing his 41.Infanterie-Division and digging in, anticipating reinforcement and resupply.

Buoyed by this news, army headquarters changed I.Armee-Korps' orders for the third time in as many hours. Instead of moving on the Mühlen See, François was now to occupy Neidenburg in strength, and after pushing Falk out towards Grünfließ, was to place himself across what would ultimately become the enemy's principal line of retreat. The town itself was firmly under German control by the early evening, but in his advance towards Grünfließ Falk was engaged by part of the 3rd Guards Division, which had spent much of the previous weeks moving up to the front line and was only reaching its destination as the battle was nearing its climax. With the Germans thwarted by an enemy cavalry screen, the fighting was ultimately short lived; after blazing away at the treeline to little or no effect, Falk disengaged to await further orders.

The timbre of the battle was now changing considerably and swinging heavily in the Germans' favour, so much so that at 1330hrs, Scholtz was ordered to attack along his entire line. Sontag, on grounds of his division's present condition, singularly refused to comply with this instruction, having fought hard against what had been, numerically at least, a superior enemy. Martos' XV Corps, however, was slowly coming to the end of its fighting ability, its resistance lessening with every passing hour.

With the khaki-clad Russian troops using up the last of their precious ammunition and seeing few alternatives, large numbers of them charged their last magazines or fixed bayonets, ready to continue the fight. Just as many began to raise their hands or display rudimentary white flags in token of surrender, Breithaupt's 70.Landwehr-Brigade took almost 2,000 prisoners almost by accident, the greatcoated infantry more than aware that there was a greater chance of food in the German lines than in the Russian ones.

With the Landwehr and reservists fighting in the centre, and Sontag adamantly refusing to take any further part in the battle, 37.Infanterie-Division now moved eastwards, before angling towards Hohenstein, the men moving at as fast a pace as their commanding general thought they could sustain whilst still being able to fight a battle once they had reached their objective. At 1500hrs, while his infantry took a much-needed water break and checked their equipment, Staabs deployed his artillery on the rising ground west of the town. The batteries came into action almost as soon as they had unlimbered, the German guns receiving the attention of every enemy artillery piece within a reasonable distance. As their comrades continued to deal out and receive punishment, the infantry prepared to take their turn in what the more cynical would eventually term the 'Spandau Ballet'. But the order never came.

Shortly after his artillery had begun to open fire, Staabs' headquarters was visited by a staff captain from Goltz's division, who brought the news that the gunners were also shelling the Landwehr; the latter had been obliged to advance in two different directions in order to protect against flank attacks from significant enemy forces. Staabs responded by saying that the new arrivals had no right to be where they were as their current position was preventing his own men from making their attack on Hohenstein. The result was such that while Staabs' troops consolidated their positions for an attack the following day, Goltz's part-time soldiers were steadily driven back by Klujew's men coming in from the east. However, just like Martos' beleaguered command to the south, Klujew's men bent and they folded, but they never broke, their determination ensuring the integrity of XX Corps' position.

Further east, it looked as if any cooperation between Mackensen and Below had ended, a dispute over seniority instigated by the former causing him to order Below 'off the road' so that the regular troops could march on Allenstein. Catastrophe, in the form of a traffic jam that would have immobilized both commands for a considerable period of time, was narrowly avoided when aerial reconnaissance indicated that the Russian VI Corps had withdrawn from the battle area and should no longer be considered a threat.

This meant that, on paper at least, the advantage had finally swung in favour of the Germans, who could now muster the equivalent of almost six corps against the three still available to Samsonov.

As commander of the lead formation, Below was ordered to proceed with the capture of Allenstein before swinging south on the Hohenstein road. He achieved this task with mixed results: whilst 1.Reserve-Division overran Klujew's baggage train, their comrades in 36.Reserve-Division had the bad luck to encounter the Russian rearguard, who fought determinedly to allow their comrades to escape, 500 men falling in a bayonet charge once their ammunition had run out.

To his relief, and with any joint action between the two formations officially over, Mackensen was ordered to move directly south towards Ortelsburg and from there to Jedwabno en route to Neidenburg. Whilst bad luck, conflicting orders and communications failure had served to bring the Russian Second Army to its present situation, these self-same considerations had also contrived to place 8.Armee's four army corps in such a position that they would now be approaching the enemy from each point of the compass.

DESTRUCTION OF AN ARMY: 29–30 AUGUST

For Samsonov, now at XV Corps headquarters, the writing was on the wall. At no stage during the battle had any of his subordinate formations fought as anything other than individual corps, and with one of them out of the battle zone, and a further one and a half more on the (for him) wrong side of the Neide, his army was reduced to two and a half badly supplied corps. Attack was no longer an option, the only chance being a staged withdrawal eastwards, enabling him to consolidate his forces and mount a credible defence until reinforced or relieved. To accomplish this, Samsonov had first to escape the very real threat of encirclement.

At around 0700hrs on 29 August, a flustered Below moved his corps along the road to Hohenstein – with uncharacteristically little regard for stragglers – before coming up hard against Russian troops entrenched around the village of Grieslienen, several miles short of his objective. As always, the Russians had proven themselves to be the masters of defence, and despite every advantage it held, it still took I.Reserve-Korps almost three hours to break down the enemy resistance.

To the south-west, Staabs and Goltz had resolved their problems with the Landwehr bypassing Hohenstein to capture the village of Mörken and cut the Russian line of retreat, whilst Staabs, after another bombardment, sent his men into the town's burning ruins to evict its Russian garrison. With 3.Reserve-Division pushing ahead south of the fighting, Klujew's XIII Corps was being hit from three sides, defending its positions with bravura and making the enemy pay heavily for every yard of ground gained. This could have been how the story played itself out, but having cleared the road and advanced some distance past Grieslienen, Below could observe the battlefield before him and brought up his entire artillery to add its support to the attack.

The devastation was immediate; but despite this, and as in other engagements of the previous days, whilst large numbers of Russians offered their surrender, just as many continued to fight on, either as units, small groups or individuals. Their continued resistance increased the 'butcher's

The situation on 29–30 August 1914

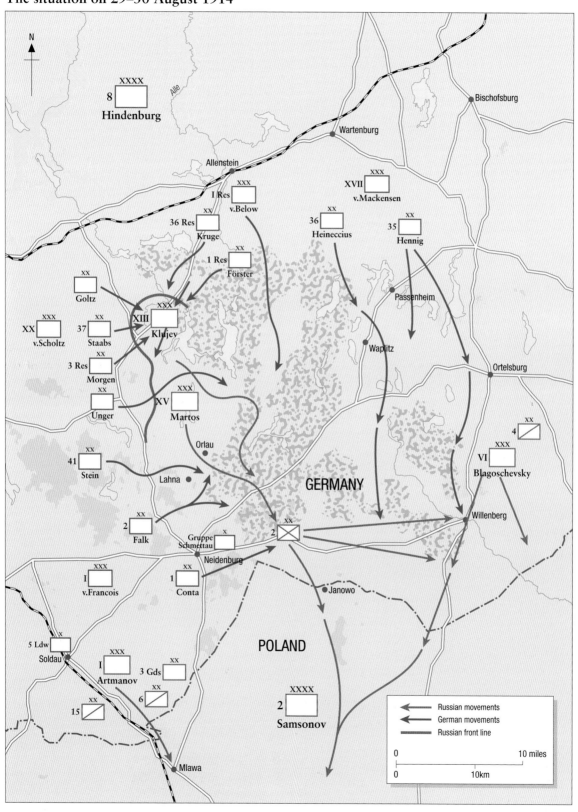

N

XXXX
8
Hindenburg

Alle

● Bischofsburg

● Wartenburg

Allenstein ●

XXX
I Res
v.Below

XXX
XVII
v.Mackensen

XX
36 Res
Kruge

XX
1 Res
Förster

XX
36
Heineccius

XX
35
Hennig

● Passenheim

XX
Goltz

XXX
XIII
Klujev

XXX
XX **v.Scholtz**

XX
37
Staabs

XX
3 Res
Morgen

XX
Unger

XXX
XV
Martos

● Waplitz

● Ortelsburg

XX
4

● Orlau

XX
41
Stein

Lahna ●

GERMANY

XXX
VI
Blagoschevsky

● Willenberg

XX
2
Falk

X
Gruppe Schmettau

XX
2

Neidenburg

XXX
I
v.Francois

XX
1
Conta

● Janowo

X
5 Ldw
Soldau

XXX
I
Artmanov

XX
3 Gds

POLAND

XX
6

XX
15

XXXX
2
Samsonov

● Mlawa

	Russian movements
	German movements
	Russian front line

0 _____ 10 miles

0 _____ 10km

UNCORKING THE BOTTLE: HOHENSTEIN, 29 AUGUST 1914 (PP. 84–85)

Originally scheduled to take place on 28 August, the planned German attack on Hohenstein had collapsed following the confused intermingling of Staabs' 37.Infanterie-Division with Goltz's Landwehr troops as they marched towards diverging objectives. The failure to take the objective gave Klujew's Russian XIII Corps a valuable strongpoint around which to conduct their defence, one which could not be bypassed and which the Germans would need to capture before they could advance further into the heart of Second Army's remaining formations. Its possession was therefore crucial to both sides.

With the logistical problems resolved, Staabs now planned to conduct a heavy bombardment of the town before committing his brigades to capturing it, whilst Goltz – as per his orders – would bypass Hohenstein and take up position on its southern flank and block any Russian relief attempts.

As the guns fell silent, and with many of Hohenstein's buildings on fire, Staabs gave the order for the attack to commence. The contending forces fought throughout the morning and into the late afternoon, house by house, street by street, building by building. The defenders gave ground unwillingly, but their

position was ultimately rendered untenable by the arrival of Below's I.Reserve-Korps from Allenstein and the commitment of his massed artillery to the battle.

Having fought their way into the town, here we see the men of Colonel Otto von Heydebreck's Infanterie-Regiment 146 (1st Masurian, **1**) being confronted by a Russian counter-attack (**2**). Daylight is all but obscured by the smoke billowing from burning buildings, both as a result of the preparatory bombardment and the Russian practice of setting light to buildings even as they were being forced from them. It was in these conditions that the hand-to-hand combat took place, with men often unable to tell friend from foe, their wounded comrades being lucky if they could be moved to safety from where they fell within the conflagration.

Eventually the German pressure began to tell. With the town virtually surrounded, it was finally recaptured by Staabs' troops. This removed the obstacle that had until now anchored the enemy position, and allowed both XX.Armee-Korps and I.Reserve-Korps to push southwards into Martos' Russian XV Corps, which was effectively holding Second Army's escape route open.

bill', but by mid-afternoon the fighting was all but over, the columns of smoke rising above the roofs of Hohenstein silent testament to the death and destruction that had occurred in the streets, houses and surrounding fields.

Still spoiling for a fight and freed of his 'shackles', Mackensen resolved to follow his orders implicitly – and woe betide anyone, friend or foe, who was unfortunate enough to stand in his way. Having retraced its earlier march, 35.Infanterie-Division was directed to move south towards Passenheim and then Jedwabno, whilst sending a strong detachment to hold the crossroads at Ortelsberg. Its running mate – 36.Infanterie-Division – was to reach the same objective by moving through Scheufelsdorf and Waplitz. Like units on both sides, XVII.Armee-Korps had suffered greatly since the Battle of Gumbinnnen, its men moving like automata, driven onwards by their officers and NCOs; but eventually, straggling became endemic, the regiments and battalions leaving dozens of men by the roadside, all of them promising to continue but simply too weak to do so. As was soon to be repeated across a wide area, the leading elements of both columns began firstly to pass broken enemy transport and equipment, then impedimenta that had been simply abandoned, and finally increasing numbers of men standing with arms raised. The adrenalin rush caused by these tangible signs of victory undoubtedly spurred the men on to further exertions before they were ordered to halt or their bodies collapsed.

With Mackensen and Below now pushing the enemy from the north and east, all that Scholtz needed to do was to maintain the western side of the box and prevent the enemy from making a breakout. With his brigades and divisions – whether active, Reserve or Landwehr – having fought themselves into the ground, he was more than happy to do so.

'Germany's pride'. Here, Kaiser Wilhelm II seeks to link himself with Hindenburg's victory at Tannenberg. (Author's collection)

Far to the south, arguably the most successful of the German commanders was wrestling with his own problems, having received two sets of orders from the high command. The first of these was to block a 20-mile line stretching from Neidenburg to Willenburg and prevent the enemy from escaping across the Narew, whilst simultaneously concentrating his forces to prevent an enemy breakout via Neidenburg. However, in attempting the former, he would undoubtedly compromise his ability to achieve the latter.

Naturally, François elected to follow only a part of his orders. He instructed Schmettau's command, supported by 1.Infanterie-Division, to advance to Muschaken, roughly halfway to Willenburg, where he was to await orders. The remaining division, under Falk, was ordered to cover Neidenburg by occupying Grünfließ, his advance being blocked by the battered remnants of the Russian 2nd Infantry Division.

Whether as a result of an inherent feeling that victory was imminent or simply the fact they had enjoyed a steep learning curve over the preceding weeks, the Landser were less than enthusiastic about rushed advances cross-country. They were more than happy to take their time and rely on artillery or machine-gun support to break up the enemy positions,

MOPPING-UP OPERATIONS NEAR SALUSKEN, 29 AUGUST 1914 (PP. 88–89)

With the German XX.Armee-Korps and I.Reserve-Korps heavily engaged against the Russian XIII Corps around Hohenstein, and with XV Corps along the Drewenz River, it fell to François' I.Armee-Korps and Mackensen's XVII.Armee-Korps to complete the developing encirclement and cut off Samsonov's possible lines of retreat to the south and the west respectively. In both cases, numerically at least, the German corps enjoyed a significant advantage over their foes, but the advance was a cautious one, the men of 8.Armee having been given – on numerous occasions since the Russian invasion of East Prussia – adequate demonstration of how tenacious their enemy could be in either attack or defence.

This scene shows the advance of Colonel Julius von Fumetti's Füsilier-Regiment 'Graf von Roon' (Ostpreußisches) 33 (**1**) from 4.Infanterie-Brigade of von Falk's 2.Infanterie-Division near the village of Salusken. Here they came into contact with the shattered remnants of Lieutenant General Alexander Dushkevich's 2nd Infantry Division (**2**) of XXIII Corps, a unit which had been mauled and battered over the preceding days' combat. It is uncertain as to exactly which of Dushkevich's four regiments were involved in the fighting at Salusken, but it would be apt if they were from his 1st Infantry Brigade: the 5th Infantry Regiment's honorary colonel being Kaiser Wilhelm I; whilst that of the 6th Infantry was Prince Friedrich-Leopold of Prussia, the Kaiser's cousin.

Advancing – as prescribed – in section groups, the German infantrymen are pushing their way through the disorganized enemy, large numbers of whom saw surrender as a sure route to survival rather than headlong flight and a possible solitary death in the strange wooded terrain over which they had fought in the previous days. The combat was far from one-sided, with 12 Germans and 32 Russians being buried locally, but nonetheless the haul of prisoners would increase over the coming days, with a reputed 60 trains being needed to transport the Russian POWs to Germany proper.

before conducting local mopping-up operations in anything up to battalion strength, preferring that another unit lead the advance and suffer the attention of any snipers that the enemy had left behind. In this manner, the Russian 2nd Division had exculpated its previous failures, their field-grey counterparts able to advance no more than three miles before night fell. A similar situation developed in François' centre when Conta's men were forced to remain close to Neidenburg for several hours whilst a series of ultimately inaccurate reports of enemy activity were investigated. While I.Armee-Korps' infantry were stalled, it fell to Ulanen-Regiment 8 to score perhaps the most important triumph of recent days. Whilst out on patrol, the regiment, supported by some Landwehr cavalry, a battery of artillery and a platoon of grenadiers, chanced upon the combined trains of both the Russian XV Corps and the 2nd Division. After a round or two of artillery fire, buglers sounded the charge and the German cavalrymen swept out of cover, scattering the convoy's escorts and capturing over 1,000 wagons and close to 5,000 prisoners.

German newspaper illustration showing the pusuit of the Russian Second Army after Tannenberg. (Author's collection)

On the road to Muschaken, Schmettau quickly overran a dispirited enemy defence. Deciding to push on to Willenburg, his progress slowed by the sheer amount of enemy *matériel* that was strewn across his path, he reached his objective at 2000hrs that evening, thereby closing the trap.

As night fell, Hindenburg and Ludendorff took stock of the scale of the victory that they had achieved. From an initial strength of a little under 200,000 men, the Russian Second Army had lost an estimated 50,000 killed, 30,000 wounded and up to 90,000 prisoners,[4] together with up to 500 pieces of artillery and countless articles of baggage, equipment and small arms. Against this, the German records show a total of 1,891 killed, 6,579 wounded and 4,588 missing from an initial strength of almost 155,000 effectives.

Back at headquarters, Hindenburg communicated the news of the victory to both the Kaiser and OHL. The initial reports referred to the 'Battle of Allenstein', as this was the largest town in the area over which the fighting had taken place. When asked by Wilhelm II how the battle should be known, Hindenburg remembered an aside by Max Hoffmann (Deputy Chief of Staff of 8.Armee) who had earlier pointed out the name of a small village that they had driven through whilst in the process of relocating the army headquarters. Although it had seen little or no fighting, it was nonetheless a name that, due to the defeat of the Teutonic Knights in 1410, had long resonated in German history – Tannenberg.

4   The records are unclear if the former are wounded POWs and the latter unwounded ones. Likewise, Russian sources tend to dispute these numbers, instead suggesting a total loss of 90,000 men.

AFTERMATH

With the recapture of Willenburg and the closing of the trap, the fighting had more or less come to an end. The remnants of the Russian XIII, XV and XXIII corps had been encircled in what would – on numerous occasions afterwards – be referred to as a 'Cannae manoeuvre', a disaster which the Second Army's I and VI corps only escaped being embroiled in as a result of their earlier defeats – ones which, it must be said, contributed greatly to the circumstances that led to the Russian disaster. Both Klujew and Martos would be captured while trying to make their way to safety, whilst Kondratovich remained at large, only to be later dismissed from his command and transferred to the staff of the Minsk Military District. Whilst attempting to escape with a small escort and cross the Narew near Willenberg, Samsonov waited until his bodyguards were asleep and then walked into the nearby woods and took his own life.

As a mark of respect, Samsonov was interred where his body was later found, and a cairn was erected over the site with a plaque which read:

General SAMSONOW der Gegner Hindenburgs in der Schlacht
bei Tannenberg
Gefallen 30.08.1914
(General Samsonov, Hindenburg's Opponent at the Battle of Tannenberg
Killed in Action 30.08.1914)

General Klujew, commander of the Russian XIII Corps, Second Army, following his capture. (Wikimedia Commons)

In 1916, and through the agency of the International Red Cross, the general's body was exhumed and his remains repatriated to his widow for reburial in Russia.

On the German side, the most immediate reaction was the acknowledgement that the Schlieffen Plan was in fact deeply flawed and that the circumstances under which it was conceived had no basis in modern warfare. Above all, it was acknowledged that the ratio between forces deployed to make the attack in the West and those used to defend East Prussia was deeply imbalanced and that an urgent reinforcement would be needed if the situation that had just been faced was to be avoided again. As a result of this, the OHL agreed to transfer two infantry corps and a cavalry division to reinforce 8.Armee. This ultimately allowed it to successfully engage and defeat Rennenkampf at the First Battle

Ten years after: the Tannenberg German generals gather at Königsberg in 1924 to mark the anniversary of the battle. (Author's collection)

of the Masurian Lakes (7–14 September 1914); the movement of troops was – according to some commentators – a factor in the German defeat at the First Battle of the Marne, which took place at almost the same time (6–12 September 1914).

As a result of their victory Hindenburg and Ludendorff would enjoy celebrity and promotion, both men effectively directing the German war effort from 1916 until the capitulation in 1918. Each would later take an active part in German politics, with Ludendorff, flirting with the nascent nationalism and right-wing politics of the post-war years, coming last in the presidential election of 1925; and Hindenburg being persuaded to come out of his second retirement to act as a 'continuity candidate' behind which the conservative parties could unite and hold off threats from both left- and right-wing parties.

Hindenburg was to serve as President of Germany from 1925 to 1933, and upon his death was buried with great ceremony at the Tannenberg Memorial, which had been dedicated on the tenth anniversary of the battle. Disinterred prior to the Soviet conquest of Poland in 1944, his body and that of his wife were later reinterred at Marburg by US forces.

The Tannenberg Memorial, dedicated on the tenth anniversary of the battle in 1924, near Hohenstein (now Olsztynek, Poland). Hindenburg was interred at the site in 1934. The memorial was later razed to the ground under Soviet occupation. (Author's collection)

SELECT BIBLIOGRAPHY

Bucholz, Frank et al, *The Great War Dawning: Germany and its Army at the Start of World War I*, Verlag Militaria, Vienna, 2013

Buttar, Prit, *Collision of Empires: The War on the Eastern Front in 1914*, Osprey Publishing, Oxford, 2014

Cornish, Nik, *The Russian Army and the First World War*, Spellmount, Stroud, 2006

Cron, Hermann, *The Imperial German Army 1914–18*, Helion & Co, Solihull, 2002

Ettighoffer, Paul C., *Tannenberg: Eine Armee wird zum Tode Marschiert*, Bertelsmann Verlag, Gütersloh, 1939

François, Hermann von, *Tannenberg: Das Cannae des Weltkrieges in Wört und Bild*, Verlag Deutscher Jägerbund, Berlin, 1926

Frerichs, Kim Oliver, *Application of Operational Art: The German 8th Army at the Battles at Tannenberg 1914*, graduate thesis, US Army Command & General Staff College, Fort Leavenworth, Kansas, 2015

Government Printing Office, *Vocabulary of German Military Terms and Abbreviations*, Washington DC, 1917

Handbook of the German Army (Fourth Edition), War Office, London, 1914

Handbook of the Russian Army (Sixth Edition), War Office, London, 1914

Herwig, Holger, *The First World War: Germany and Austria-Hungary 1914–1918*, Arnold Publishing, London, 1997

Histories of the 251 Divisions of the German Army which Participated in the War (1914–1918), Washington DC, 1920

Hoffmann, Carl A.M., *War Diaries*, two volumes, Naval & Military Press, Uckfield, 2004

Imperial General Staff Field Service Regulations of the German Army (translated), War Office, London, 1908

Jackson, Frederick E., *Tannenberg: The First Use of Signals Intelligence in Modern Warfare*, US Army War College, Carlisle Barracks, Pennsylvania, 2002

Knox, Alfred, *With the Russian Army 1914–1917*, two volumes, Hutchinson, London, 1921

Kürenberg, Joachim von, *Russlands Weg nach Tannenberg*, Büchergilde Gütenberg, Berlin, 1934

Kuropatkin, Alexei N., *The Russian Army and the Japanese War*, two volumes, John Murray, London, 1909

Linde, Paul, *Gegen Rennenkampf und Joffre*, Xenien Verlag, Leipzig, 1915

Littauer, Vladimir, *Russian Hussar: A Story of the Imperial Cavalry 1911–1920*, White Mane Publishing Co., Shippensburg, Pensylvannia, 1993

Ludendorff, Erich, *Ludendorff's Own Story*, two volumes, Harper & Brothers, New York, 1919

——, *Meine Kriegserinnerungen: 1914–1918*, Mittler & Sohn, Berlin, 1919

Ludwig, Emil, *Hindenburg and the Saga of the German Revolution*, William Heinemann Ltd, London, 1935

Neumann, Georg Paul, *The German Air Force in the Great War*, Hodder & Stoughton, London, 1920

Noonan, Robert S., *Tannenberg and the Principles of War: A Historical Battle Analysis*, graduate thesis, US Air Command and Staff College, Maxwell Air Force Base, Alabama, 1984

Pares, Bernard, *Day by Day with the Russian Army 1914–15*, Constable & Co., London, 1915

Rangliste der Königlich Preußichen Armee und des XIII (Königlich Württembergichen) Armeekorps – Stand 06.05.1914 Kaiserliches Kriegsministerium, Berlin, 1914

Rehwaldt, Hermann, *Tannenberg Rettet Ostpreussen*, Bischof und Klein, Lengerich, 1930

Schäfer, Theobald von, *Die Schlacht bei Tannenberg 1914*, Oldenburg i.D., Berlin, 1927

Schulz, Hugo F.W., *Die Preussichen Kavallerie-Regimenter 1913/1914*, Weltbild Verlag, Augsburg, 1992

Showalter, Dennis, *Tannenberg: Clash of Empires, 1914*, Brassey's Inc., Dulles, Virginia, 2004

——, *Instrument of War: The German Army 1914–18*, Osprey Publishing, Oxford, 2016

Solzhenitsyn, Alexander, *August 1914*, Bodley Head, London, 1971

Steveni, William Barnes, *The Russian Army from Within*, George H. Doran Company, New York, 1914

Stone, David, *The Kaiser's Army: The German Army in World War One*, Bloomsbury, London, 2015

——, *The Russian Army in the Great War: The Eastern Front 1914–17*, University Press of Kansas, Lawrence, Kansas, 2015

Sweetman, John, *Tannenberg 1914*, Cassell & Co., London, 2002

Tannenberg: Gesichtliche Wahrheit über die Schlacht, Ludendorff Verlag, Munich, 1939

Volkmann, Erich O., *Strategischer Atlas zum Weltkrieg*, Bibliographisches Insitut AG, Leipzig, 1937

Wenninger, Karl Ritter von, *Die Schlacht von Tannenberg*, Ludendorff Verlag, Munich, 1935

Wentzler, Sebastian, *Die Schütte-Lanz Innovation: Technische Neuerungen des Luftschiffbaus Schütte-Lanz in den Jahren 1909–14 im Vergleich zum Luftschiffbau Zeppelin*, Bibliotheks- und Informationssystem der Universität Oldenburg, 2000

Wie der Weltkrieg 1914 'gemacht' wurde, Ludendorff Verlag, Munich, 1934

INDEX